Mother & Child

FOREWORD

A New Little Person

Congratulations! You have been given a little child, a completely new, unique little person on this planet. And this person will make his or her own very special mark on this world. Not least it will effect you, your life, and the life of others around you! To be a parent is the most important and the most complex task we pursue in our lives. A task most of us do not have any previous experience in carrying out. But a task which we cannot neglect. In the beginning especially, it may seem incredible that such a little bundle can occupy at least one adult person around the clock, day in day out. And it may also seem incredible that this tiny human being can make you feel so much!

The rewards for your dedication will be many—like the first time your baby looks at you, the first smile, the first steps. You'll experience the miracle of a tiny human being as your baby's body and mind undergo an amazingly rapid development during the first year—a year when the foundation for so many things is built. You'll experience a little person who will move you deeply and change your life forever.

The goal of Mother & Child is not to be a manual for good parenting. However, it is full of useful tips and advice regarding a range of subjects that will concern you especially during the first year of your baby's life. You will find useful information about important subjects such as infant care, breast-feeding, your baby's physical and psychological development, and health checkups and immunizations. We have also included information about the importance of touch, closeness, and safety.

To make sure that Mother & Child is as accurate and as current as possible, all of the chapters were written and reviewed by doctors, midwives, and other health professionals.

This book is organized so that you can read it from beginning to end, and then use it as a reference book. If you are looking for a particular subject, you will find a Table of Contents on pages 3 through 5 and a thorough index on pages 116 through 119.

If there is something you cannot find an answer to, or if you have suggestions for new topics, please write to us at the address below. We would also be glad to receive any other comments about this book.

Mother & Child Editorial Offices
1 Pearl Buck Court
Bristol, PA 19007

We hope that <u>Mother & Child</u> will be a source of both pleasure and useful knowledge. And we wish you the greatest joy on the new addition to your life!

IMPORTANT NOTE: This book is intended to give general information. It should not take the place of the advice of your own doctor and other health professionals. The authors, editors, advisors, and publishers of this book cannot be held responsible for any errors or omissions herein.

Revised and reprinted 1999, 2000. (3rd. time.)
Copyright © This Edition 1999
Baby's First Book Club®
Bristol, PA 19007

Copyright © 1995 Sandvik Publishing, Bristol, PA 19007

Printed in Italy.
ISBN 1-58048-051-9

Table of Contents

CHAPTER 6:

Allergies

CHAPTER 7:

Colic

CHAPTER 8:

Baby Massage

CHAPTER 9:

Baby Care

CHAPTER 10:

Baby Clothes and Equipment

CHAPTER 11:

Baby Shoes

CHAPTER 12:

Physical Growth and Development

CHAPTER 13:

Psychological Development

CHAPTER 14:

Baby's Checkups and Immunizations

CHAPTER 15:

When Baby's Sick

CHAPTER 16:

In Safe Hands

Advisory Council

Barbara J. Bason

Ms. Bason is a certified childbirth educator, health educator, and homeopathy assistant in Wilmington, Delaware. She received bachelor's degrees in biology and in medical technology from the University of Delaware, and has since received training in childbirth education and assistance, counseling of nursing mothers, post-partum care, midwifery, prenatal and postnatal aquatic fitness, and homeopathy.

Ms. Bason co-founded and directed the non-profit Informed Birth of Delaware, and has volunteered for Nursing Mothers, Inc. since 1984. She lectures widely for the March of Dimes' Babies and You program and for other groups. Ms. Bason is a member of the Northern Delaware Homeopathic Study Group and is registered with the American Society of Clinical Pathologists.

Patrick S. Pasquariello, Jr., M.D.

Dr. Pasquariello is professor of pediatrics at the Children's Hospital of Philadelphia and at the University of Pennsylvania School of Medicine. He also directs the Medical Education Center and the Diagnostic Center at Children's Hospital. His medical degree is from Jefferson Medical College.

Dr. Pasquariello is certified by the American Board of Pediatrics. He is a fellow of the American Academy of Pediatrics, the American College of Physicians, and the Philadelphia College of Physicians. He has held editorial, academic, and con-sulting positions, and is widely published.

Jeffrey P. Phelan, M.D., J.D.

Dr. Phelan is co-director of maternal-fetal medicine in the Department of Obstetrics and Gynecology at Pomona Valley Hospital and San Antonio Community Hospital in California. He received his medical degree from the University of Miami School of Medicine and his law degree from Loyola Law School. In medicine, he is certified in obstetrics and gynecology and in maternal-fetal medicine.

Dr. Phelan has appeared on television and radio, and has given testimony before government agencies such as the FDA. He was also named Best Doctor in America in 1994—1995. Dr. Phelan is a member of the American College of Obstetricians and Gynecologists, the Society of Perinatal Obstetricians, and the American College of Legal Medicine.

Debra L. Somers, M.D.

Dr. Somers is a partner in a large obstetrics and gynecology practice in Philadelphia and Elkins Park, Pennsylvania. She received her medical degree from the Thomas Jefferson Medical College and then specialized in obstetrics and gynecology for her internship and residency at Western Pennsylvania Hospital in Pittsburgh.

Dr. Somers is certified by the National Board of Medical Examiners, and is a junior fellow of the American College of Obstetricians and Gynecologists. She also is a member of the American Association of Gynecologic Laparoscopists and the American Society for Colposcopy and Cervical Pathology.

Marsden Wagner, M.D., M.S.P.H.

Dr. Wagner is a private consultant in women's and children's health and perinatal epidemiology throughout the world. He received his medical degree and his master's degree in public health from the University of California at Los Angeles.

Dr. Wagner previously taught at the University of California at Los Angeles. He co-directed the Bureau of Maternal and Child Health for the California Department of Public Health, and was responsible for women's and children's health for 33 countries on behalf of the World Health Organization. Dr. Wagner has had over 80 scientific articles and five books published, and he lectures worldwide.

Publication designed by Dorland Sweeney Jones, Philadelphia, Pa.

CHAPTER 1

In the Beginning

THE IMPORTANCE OF INTERPLAY BETWEEN MOTHER AND CHILD

We know today that newborn babies enter the world as complete little people who can see, hear, smell, taste, and feel. They are *not* passive and uninterested, as people used to think. Even immediately after birth, babies are interested in their environment and are sensitive to stimulation. When newborns are put onto their mother's tummy, they'll often look up at her with curiosity. Through eye contact, hugging, kissing, talking, and loving touch, the earliest bonds are formed. These kinds of contact help babies develop into people who are comfortable with their surroundings.

Because of all that, it's important that the interplay between mother and child start as soon after birth as possible. The baby is physically separate from you for the first time ever, so it's best if the two of you can have a little peace and quiet, gliding softly and naturally into a *new* kind of togetherness.

Your feeling of "motherly instinct" and responsibility will grow with your ability to interpret and respect your baby's signals. And because you will be helping your child interpret the world, it's very important that you convey trust, hope, and love.

BEING IN RHYTHMIC HARMONY

Even if you work outside the home, you'll probably be the person who looks after your baby the most and is closest to him or her during the early years. Through feeding and continual care, you will learn what your child's facial expressions, movements, and cries mean. You'll become more and more receptive to your child's rhythms for eating, sleeping, and being awake.

People who research these things sometimes talk about the mother-child interplay as being as synchronized and rhythmic as a dance. You and your child should "waltz" together — the child gives signals and you answer, you give signals and the child answers. It's also good if your partner can bond with the baby in this way.

In the beginning, the "synchronization" often takes place through long periods of eye contact, for example at the end of each feeding. One of you makes eye contact, and you gradually move the baby to your lap, your knees bent, with his or her head lying in both your hands. In this "en face position," your eyes are on the same level. The two of you can sit together for long periods and communicate through eye contact and soothing sounds and touch.

LOVING TOUCH

Infants are particularly aware of touch, so a gentle massage is a great way to communicate with your baby. A gentle massage will relax both of you and join your "rhythms." Others can do this, too, as a nice way of bonding.

When the baby is waking up from a deep sleep, but is still not completely awake, you can pick him or her carefully up into your lap. Put the baby skin-to-skin with you and stroke the back or all over the body. When you do this, you should be in a comfortable position — perhaps in bed, in a rocking chair, or in a good reclining chair — maybe with some relaxing music in the background.

Skin contact affects the nerves in the skin, releasing hormones — including your breast hormones. The hormones will calm the two of you, and could even help breast-feeding. If your baby shows signs of being hungry, do go ahead and feed him or her.

"THIRD-DAY BLUES"

Even after you give birth, and while you breast-feed, your hormones will be adjusting themselves. The powerful hormonal shifts can affect you physically and emotionally. One common effect is called "third-day blues." You might start crying for no apparent reason, even if you're not really unhappy! This is quite natural — especially during the first several days after giving birth. These feelings usually go away after a few days, though they may come back at times when you're very tired or sad. But if you feel that it's all becoming too difficult and there are too many times with the blues, please talk to your doctor or another trusted advisor — it might be a sign of a more serious problem. You'll feel better if someone you feel comfortable with — a friend, relative, or trained doula — can help you with cooking and other household chores.

FEELING ISOLATED

With all of the advantages we have in this country, modern life has also brought some disadvantages. One that you're likely to encounter is that our "social network" has changed. People have gotten more mobile. Long distances and different work schedules separate relatives and friends. If you're staying home with the baby, you could feel very isolated at first...You might not see or talk to another adult for 10 or 12 hours a day! After having lived an active, sociable life, you enter a period where you may feel quite confined in your home, particularly right after other people have gone to work in the morning.

As a modern woman, you have another disadvantage in relation to your ancestors: You may not have had as much opportunity to care for (or even to change the diaper of) a baby before. In one study, researchers asked one hundred new, first-time mothers whether they could remember the last time they had held an infant in their arms. *Over 70 of them* answered that they couldn't remember if they ever had! In the old days, there was always someone nearby who could lend support — the mother, grandmother, or neighbor. Today, you might have to call your doctor or clinic if you are worried about even something "simple." But remember...Do what makes you comfortable, even if it means calling around until you get an answer. Read as much as you can, to put your mind at ease. And look for the companionship of other new mothers through women's resource centers, mothers' support groups, and other groups.

POSTPARTUM DEPRESSION

There is a condition called "postpartum depression," which means "after-birth depression." Doctors have known for a long time that the previously mentioned "third-day tears" are related to hormones. That problem has largely been solved by explaining to new mothers what is happening to their body.

Postpartum depression, however, is different. The mother is sad, cries easily, and feels "down" almost all the time. She may also have problems eating and sleeping. This can continue for weeks or months, in which case she needs a doctor or therapist to help her emerge from the depression. If this happens to you, find a trusted health care professional to whom you can express all your thoughts and feelings about being a new mother. It'll help you regain your "balance," and will let you convey a positive outlook to your baby in his or her first precious months. For more information, talk to your doctor, midwife, or childbirth educator, or check the Yellow Pages to find self-help groups near you. Also, see Chapter 2. "Postpartum Depression," on pages 14 to 15.

COLICKY BABIES

Babies need to learn how to adapt to life outside the womb. Sleeping newborns are sort of the way they were inside the womb. Their sleep is interrupted every now and then, in a more or less regular way, for physical needs. Hunger and discomfort, pain and crying are satisfied by feeding and changing, tenderness, closeness, and sleep. Gradually, a rhythm of sleep and activity develop. Some children, however, find it hard to find a rhythm, so they cry and cry, and can't fall asleep — which puts quite a strain on them and their parents. If a child has frequent, powerful crying spells, pulls the legs up, makes the hands into fists, and can't be consoled, we call it colic. This is discussed in Chapter 7, "Colic," on pages 45 to 47.

THE MOST NATURAL INCUBATOR IS THE MOTHER

It may seem a paradox that we sometimes have to turn to science, only to rediscover natural things. Premature birth usually means that mother and baby will be separated for a while. The baby is put into an incubator to monitor and help him or her. Unfortunately, this also means that the preemie missed out on a lot of the early stimulation and bonding that full-term babies get.

However, there is an alternative to the incubator, if the baby is in good shape — the mother herself! Hospitals in Colombia, in South America, have been trying "the kangaroo method" for several years. In the kangaroo method, the healthy preemie is put onto the mother as soon as possible — under her blouse, between her breasts, in an upright position, like a baby kangaroo in its mother's pouch. The baby stays this way, day and night, to receive warmth, nourishment, and nurturing. Not only have more of the preemies survived and thrived, but the new mothers have gained self confidence, as well. *They*, not the hospital, helped their babies! Now, hospitals in the United States and other industrialized countries have also used this method and, after careful testing, found it to be generally safe.

CHAPTER 2

Postpartum Depression

WHAT IS POSTPARTUM DEPRESSION?

Having children triggers difficult feelings for many women. You might have trouble sleeping; become irritable, restless, and anxious; and develop an overwhelming need to cry. About half of all women who have recently given birth experience some postpartum blues. Interestingly, researchers haven't been able to find any clear differences in the hormone levels of women who do get severe postpartum tears and women who don't. For most new mothers, the weepiness will disappear after a few days. If it lasts considerably longer, it's called postpartum depression.

WHY AM I DEPRESSED WHEN MY LIFE IS SO GOOD?

Feeling overwhelmed and "depressed" can be a natural reaction to giving birth. Your life has changed deeply, permanently, and quickly. Suddenly, life is ruled by the needs of the baby, and people are paying a lot more attention to him or her than to you. Your own desires must be put aside. Your new responsibilities may seem weighty. Keep in mind that men can experience similar depressions related to birth, too!

During the last part of pregnancy, you were functioning primarily on an emotional level. The moodiness and other feelings can last a while after birth, too. They are part of an important process in learning to feel compassion for the baby. If you feel vulnerable, it's easier to relate to the *infinite* vulnerability of the new baby. When giving birth, there are some risks in the situation, even if everything is apparently going smoothly. You are forced to confront your own mortality and to give yourself over to forces you cannot control and people you may not know very well. This can make anyone feel vulnerable!

A change of consciousness sometimes takes place. Many women — and men — experience it very strongly during and right after birth. It's often described as "time standing still," "time and space disappearing," or "being in a different world." You may feel like you're losing all your reference points to yourself, or you don't really know who you are. Comfort yourself in the fact that it is *not* a sign that you've "gone crazy"... it can be a very positive experience, in fact. You may feel that you value life more, and take the trouble to maintain relationships with other people.

A lot of the time, life seems pretty ideal, but the new mother struggles with postpartum blues for weeks and months. You might feel defeated... "I should be happy"... "I wanted a child"... "I have everything I want"... but blaming yourself only makes the depression worse.

So, what gives rise to such emotions when everything is seemingly fine? We've seen that different conditions can cause women — and men — to face unknown parts of themselves. Birth brings us feelings of greatness and wonder. This may be overwhelming and, unable to use words, tears may become the only expression.

WHY IS MY FAMILY MAKING ME FEEL EVEN WORSE?

If you think about it, it makes sense that other people might not understand your condition. Your family probably feels helpless. In their concern to help make things better, they might tell you to pull yourself together and look positively at the situation. Unfortunately, their attempts to "fix things" might just make you feel guilty. Try very hard to remember that your feelings are scary, but are probably normal. Try, too, to find someone willing to listen to your feelings, and help you understand how to grow from the experience.

It doesn't help that your sleep is disrupted when you have a new baby. Many new mothers feel terrible when the baby is struggling to learn that night is night. And, it's easier for conflicts in partnerships to begin when both people are suffering from lack of sleep. Everyone will need time and space to adjust to the new situation.

THE NEED FOR THERAPY

If you feel that your problems are becoming too difficult to solve, you should talk to an outsider as soon as possible. Sometimes all that's needed is to talk it out! The earlier you face the crisis, the sooner you can understand the pain and move on. Various doctors, therapists, counselors, clinics, and support groups are available to help new parents. *Don't be ashamed to use them— that's why they're there!* Time, patience, and having good help available is usually the best medicine. And remember, feeling deeply can help you be more sensitive to yourself and others.

CHAPTER 3

Physical Activities and Sex

Exercising after pregnancy has become very popular over the past few years. There are postnatal classes in most communities, and many books exist. But it's important to know what types of exercise are best for you.

You'll need to use calm movements for the first 6 months after the birth, and make sure that you don't overburden your legs. Avoid aerobics (jumping), cross-country skiing (long steps on one leg), and racquetball or competitive tennis (sudden turns). *The purpose of exercising should be well-being and toning, not training.*

THE FIRST 6 WEEKS

Most importantly: *Get enough rest and start walking!* During this period, your body will benefit the most from normal, daily movements. It should be okay for you to start a daily walking routine. Keep in mind that your body has been through a lot over the past 9 months! Don't exercise your stomach muscles yet; they will start toning up on their own. *No sit-ups!* The muscles are still very stretched, which puts an extra pressure on the weakened pelvic floor. It's probably fine to walk, but don't overdo — only do what's comfortable for you.

Lie on your stomach and rest when you can. If your breasts feels tender, put a cushion under them to relieve the pressure. This position helps to empty the uterus.

Pelvic floor exercises, or Kegel exercises, can be started right after the birth. The pelvic floor muscles are the muscles that form the "floor" under your stomach. If the pelvic floor muscles are weak, you might experience discomforts such as:

- Bladder control problems
- Gassiness
- Hemorrhoids
- Digestive problems, like constipation

- Unsatisfactory sex
- Back pain and tiredness in the lower abdomen and thighs

Pelvic floor exercises can be done anytime and anywhere, sitting or standing. Imagine that you are pulling an elevator up inside your vagina, up your abdomen. Use the muscles inside you to do the job. Hold the contraction for as long as is comfortable. If your muscles tremble, relax before doing it again. As you're pulling the elevator up, you can stop at certain points — like different floors — without coming all the way down. Imagine that you're keeping the "first-floor" muscles curved into a smile. Keep all your other muscles relaxed, and focus on the elevator. You can test your pelvic floor muscles by trying to stop the stream of urine when you're emptying your bladder. If you can do that, your muscles are well toned.

GOOD POSITIONS FOR PELVIC FLOOR EXERCISES

The positions listed below help you make the most of these exercises. You should choose the positions that are most comfortable for you. It's also important to remember to breathe! If you get hot and sweaty, feel nauseous, or get <u>palpitations</u> of the heart, stop immediately. If the feeling doesn't go away quickly, call your doctor.

1. Stand with your legs apart. Put your hands on your buttocks to make sure that your bottom doesn't tighten when you move the "elevator" up and down.
2. Lie on your stomach with one leg raised above the floor, behind you. Pull your pelvic floor muscles up and in.
3. Stand on your knees with your feet together but your knees apart. Put your arms on the floor and rest your head on them. Pull the elevator up inside your vagina.
4. Sit with your legs crossed. Keep your back straight and lean back on your hands. Pull your pelvic floor muscles up and in.
5. Stand up with knees and hips bent. Keep your back straight, and support yourself with your hands on your thighs. Pull the muscles up and in.

You don't need to get into any of these positions to do the exercises. You can do them anytime — while driving the car, feeding the baby, lying in bed, washing dishes, and so on. Also make sure to use your pelvic floor muscles when you lift heavy objects.

AFTER 6 WEEKS

You might be able to slowly start to do sit-ups. Here are some other suggestions for exercises to increase your sense of well-being:

1. Lie on your back, with your knees bent. Tighten your pelvic floor muscles. Pull in your stomach, and press the middle

of your back down on the floor. Hold this position for 5 seconds.

2. Do Exercise #1, adding rapid, tilting movements with your pelvis. This will loosen a tight back and help you regain your "pre-pregnancy" posture.
3. Lie on your back, knees bent. Tighten the pelvic floor muscles. Stretch your arms forward and lift your head from the floor. Hold for 5 seconds, then rest.
4. Exercise #3 can also be done while tilting your legs, together to one side and then the other side. This helps tone the abdominal muscles. You should not do this exercise if you feel pain in the pelvis.
5. Lie on your stomach. Tighten the pelvic floor muscles and lift your head and shoulders. Hold for at least 4 seconds. Keep your legs together the whole time.
6. Sit down, or lie on your back. Bend your ankles backward and forward. In a standing position, you can go up and down on your toes, carefully maintaining your balance. This is good if you tend to stand a lot and your ankles get swollen. If your legs are swollen, rest them on a chair or footstool when you are sitting.

AFTER 2 TO 6 MONTHS

If you don't experience any physical discomforts, you can increase your activity after 2 to 6 months. Your pelvic floor itself — and your health advisors — can guide you as to when you're ready to start more exercises. Start by walking or light jogging, to see how "tight" you are. (Empty your bladder beforehand.)

LIFTING

In your daily routine, you probably do a lot of lifting without even realizing it. You lift the baby from laps, floors, changing tables, and cribs. You carry groceries and move objects. Every time you lift something, you use your abdominal muscles, which is training in itself. However, lifting puts extra stress on the pelvic floor muscles, so try to tighten and lift at the same time. Remember to keep your back straight, while keeping your knees and hips loose.

Because your pelvis is weak for a while after you give birth, your back is particularly vulnerable. Be careful not to carry extra weight on one side of your body. Distribute the weight of groceries, books, laundry, and so forth equally to each side. If you are carrying a toddler, keep the child close to you, in front of your body, with his or her legs around your waist. This will help you avoid twisting your back or hips.

WHAT ABOUT SEX?

Sex after giving birth is experienced in different ways by different women. What seems like a chore for one woman could be a joyful reunion for another. How you experience sex depends on your own health; your sexuality; how you feel about your partner; and your feelings about pregnancy, birth, and motherhood.

The most common change in sexuality after pregnancy and birth is to feel less desire. Your erotic energy, which used to be focused around the man, might now be focused on caring for and feeling close to the baby. You might feel just too tired to even think about sex. Or, breasts full of milk, stretch marks, and a few extra pounds might make you feel unsure of whether you're still attractive. Some women feel that the birth has made their vagina too wide for satisfying intercourse. Such doubts can happen even if your partner tells you that you're as lovely as ever. Your partner's attitude during the pregnancy, and his participation in the care and responsibility for the baby, will also influence your sexual feelings.

A woman's sexual desires can be low for a number of months after the birth. For some couples, this isn't a major issue. The man may be feeling tired and strained by his new responsibilities, too, and he might not have the energy. Or, some men are confident in their feelings of inner security and understanding for their partner, and wait patiently for life to return to normal. But when your sexual needs are very different, conflicts can emerge. If your partner feels rejected, try to reassure him that though life isn't "the same" anymore, your lack of desire for sex probably won't last long. If the situation is putting a strain on the relationship, talk to your partner. If things don't improve, you might consider talking to a professional.

Allow yourself time and space to enjoy the sexual feelings that build up. And, try to *make* time for an intimate relationship with your partner. For most women, resuming a sexual life will happen naturally — it's only a matter of time.

CHAPTER 4

Breast-Feeding and Bottle-Feeding

Babies grow very quickly during the first year of life. It is particularly important, therefore, that they get good nutrition during this period. As a parent, you'll need to provide your child with healthful and complete nutrition.

BREAST-FEEDING

Throughout history, children have been breast-fed. But during the twentieth century, the number of people breast-feeding declined in many places, including North America. Luckily, breast-feeding has become more popular again. There are a number of breast-feeding organizations that offer free help and advice. Ask your doctor, midwife, childbirth educator, or local health department, or check the Yellow Pages for information.

MOTHER'S MILK: NUTRITION FOR INFANTS

Mother's milk alone is the best nutrition during the first 6 months of life, and may continue to be best for 3 months beyond that. Depending on your climate and your doctor, you may be told to supplement your breast milk with vitamin D, often in the form of cod-liver oil. Mother's milk contains enough of all the other vitamins.

The traditional recommendations about iron are being debated. As long as the baby is only receiving mother's milk, iron supplements are probably unnecessary. This applies to babies who were healthy and of normal birth weight. When you start giving your baby other foods (mixed nutrition), the amount of breast milk will start to decline, so the baby will receive less iron from breast milk. In addition, iron in other foods is not very well absorbed, so any cereals or other foods should be enriched with iron.

The nutrients in your milk are geared to the growth pattern of your infant. To accommodate rapid development of the brain, but slow growth of muscles and bones, mother's milk provides *a lot of* carbohydrates and polyunsaturated fats, but *fewer* proteins and minerals. But nutritional quantities are only one side of the coin. It's just as important that what babies eat be easily digested and absorbed. Iron is absorbed over 20 times more easily from mother's milk than from formula. So, mother's milk gives children good nutrition and, at the same time, leaves little extra stuff for intestinal bacteria to feed on.

Mother's milk contains a lot of water, so it looks bluish and "thin," sort of like skim milk. The water protects the baby against dehydration. In hot climates and during fever, a baby's kidneys put less water out into the urine. Under those physical "stresses," it's a great advantage that mother's milk doesn't burden the baby with unnecessary amounts of salt and proteins.

MOTHER'S MILK: PROTECTION AGAINST DISEASE

Mother's milk also protects your baby against bacteria and viruses that can make him or her sick. For this reason, the recent decline of breast-feeding caused a lot of illness and death among infants in countries that couldn't offer good health care. Good research also shows that babies in industrialized countries like the United States have fewer illnesses if they're breast-fed.

Mother's milk counteracts infection in two ways. First, it regulates the growth of bacteria in the baby's "gut" and intestines. Breast-fed babies' feces smell sour, but they are less irritating to the baby's skin than the feces of bottle-fed children. Second, mother's milk contains antibodies that help protect against viruses and bacteria. This gives breast-fed babies good protection against infectious diarrhea and vomiting.

COLOSTRUM: A GOOD START

The early nursings provide your baby with colostrum, which is in your breasts even before you give birth. Colostrum is yellowish and seems "richer" and more nutritious. Colostrum does contain high concentrations of antibodies that help suppress dangerous bacteria, and colostrum is easy for the newborn to digest. These are two reasons that infants should be put to the breast as soon as possible after birth.

THE PREMATURE BABY

Breast milk is at least as important for preemies as for full-term babies. But these small children — from birth — will probably need supplements of calcium, phosphate, protein, trace elements, and (after 6 weeks) iron. Your doctor will tell you what's right for your baby.

IMMEDIATELY AFTER BIRTH

Starting good routines right away is important for successful breast-feeding. The World Health Organization and UNICEF have developed certain recommendations for breast-feeding, which include:

- Put the baby to the breast as soon as possible.
- Let mother and baby be together at all hours.
- Do not give water, sugar, and so on (even formula!) to a breast-feeding newborn, unless it's medically necessary.

Midwives and childbirth educators should be able to give you guidance about breast-feeding. They should encourage feeding on demand, too (explained below).

After a normal birth, the newborn is very alert for a few hours. The baby wants to suck, and you are probably ready to start bonding. If possible, try to start breast-feeding in the first half-hour after the birth. That way, the infant will quickly receive the important colostrum. And the more frequently the baby feeds, the sooner the amount of milk will increase, and the sooner the baby will gain weight.

One of the most important duties of the father or birth partner in the time right after birth is to protect the breast-feeding woman from too many visitors, demands, and strains, which can disturb breast-feeding.

FEEDING "ON DEMAND"

In the old days, infants had their mother's breast within reach most of the time. They fed several times an hour during the day, and once or more at night. Babies want to feed that frequently because their brains need a continual supply of energy, which can't be stored for very long in youngsters. So, an infant's stomach shouldn't be empty for long periods.

Self-regulation (or feeding "on demand") means that *the baby* decides when to feed — you don't set a schedule. Your child probably knows instinctively how to control his or her feeding, and in time you can learn to interpret the different sounds and signals. Concepts like "discipline" and "spoiled" don't belong in the infant's world. Careful guidance toward a certain order, regularity, and routine, however, is fine.

Feeding on demand gives the baby security and well-being — by gaining a sense of accomplishment, and by learning that adults are responsive and trustworthy. Breast-fed children will want varying amounts of milk from one feeding to the next. So, they'll signal hunger at different intervals. This is quite normal.

Self-regulation makes it possible for the mother to adjust the amount of her milk to the baby's needs. Generally, the more the baby sucks, the faster the breasts will produce more milk. If the baby has taken — or been given — too little milk, he or she will demand more frequent meals, and you will produce more milk.

Night-time feedings

Feeding during the night is the biologically normal thing to do. In some cases, the breast milk will start to dry up without night-time feedings. It is *not* true that feeding your baby at night will damage the teeth — antibacterial substances in mother's milk will protect them. What *can* damage the teeth, however, is to let a baby lie at night with a bottle of juice or formula in the mouth.

Weaning

The length of time that infants should live on mother's milk alone is under debate. Newer research shows that children 6 to 12 months old have about a 20% lower need for energy than the World Health Organization and UNICEF had earlier assumed. So, children are probably best served by mother's milk alone (except for any vitamin D supplement) for at least 6 months. Only at around 9 months of age might they need some other foods.

Weaning and introducing mixed nutrition should, therefore, start in the second half of the first year. You should let the baby help decide the timing. Breast-feeding needn't be stopped just because the teeth start to appear. It's fine to continue with some breast-feedings into the second year of life or longer, as long as mother and baby are happy with it.

Breast-feeding techniques

It is important to put a breast-feeding baby into a good position. Turn the baby toward you so that the neck is straight and he or she doesn't have to turn the head or bend forward. Put the baby on the breast so that the nipple and a large part of the areola (darker area) go into the mouth along the roof of the mouth. The baby should suck with wide-open jaws — only then is the milk effectively massaged out of the tissue under the areola. The nipple itself is then being pulled quite a long way toward the throat. Try not to let the baby suck on your nipple with pursed lips — it'll be painful for you.

If milk doesn't start dripping out just as the baby is latching on, it may be helpful to stroke your breasts toward your nipples, with your hand, until the milk comes. This let-down reflex can be temporarily weakened if you're worried or tense. In that case, it will usually be enough to stroke the breasts.

A good position for *you* is lying on your side with a good pillow under your head. (Don't put your shoulders on the pillow.)

Bend your lower arm and rest it so that your hand is level with your head. Lay the baby under your armpit, nice and close to your body. When you use this position, your body can rest, which makes breast-feeding easier.

How long should the baby breast-feed?

For how long should the baby feed at each breast? How frequently? Should the baby be given both breasts at each feeding? Opinions differ widely, so mother and child will have to experiment. Self-regulation gives room for a lot of variety.

A good starting point is to make sure that your breasts don't become too full. If they over-fill, you'll have to empty the breasts completely. Women with a strong let-down reflex will give most of their milk in 10 minutes. For other women, it might take twice that long. Let the child stay latched on until he or she lets go of the breast, and offer the other breast. If the child doesn't want it (or has fallen asleep), and the second breast is uncomfortably full, you will have to express — or massage out — some milk, and offer that breast *first* next time.

Most infants adjust to a pattern of feeding every 2 to 4 hours during the day, and may want to feed more in the afternoons. The more frequent the meals, the less important it is to give both breasts at the same feeding.

How much breast milk should the baby get?

The child's well-being is the surest sign that he or she is getting enough milk. This can be checked by steady weight gain and good growth. But remember, half of all healthy children are *below* the average weight and length for their age, and the other half are *above*!

"Too little milk"

It's very rare that you really cannot provide enough milk — if you and your baby practice self-regulation. Breast size doesn't affect a woman's ability to breast-feed. Even if you're small-breasted, you'll probably be able to breast-feed your baby.

Some women do have a slow let-down reflex, and others produce less milk when under stress. It takes many days before the milk completely disappears — initially it's only the let-down reflex that is weakened. If you know this, you'll become less fearful of losing the milk.

If you're having trouble, try stroking your nipples a little until the milk comes. If you've had plastic surgery done to your breasts, the nipples may be less sensitive, and some of the milk ducts may have been cut. But even then, don't give up until you've tried good feeding techniques, frequent feeding, and seeking the advice of a breast-feeding advisor.

SORE NIPPLES

The best treatment for sore nipples is to try to avoid it. The baby should not latch on to your breast with his or her mouth and jaws around the nipple itself. Instead, the baby should open the mouth wide and suck the areola and underlying tissue backward toward the throat.

After the feeding, the breast should air dry with milk still on it. Don't wash the breast with soap or disinfectants. And, keeping your hands clean is important.

Creams have not proven to be useful in preventing sore nipples, nor has any form of toughening or stretching of the nipples before the birth.

MASTITIS

It's important to avoid too much pressure of milk in the breasts. If the milk is held in too long, it will start seeping out into the breast tissue, and could result in an inflammation called mastitis. This is not an infection to start with, so it shouldn't be treated with antibiotics unless it continues. Usually, part of the milk gland becomes overfilled. When that happens, the breast becomes tender, the skin gets red and warm, and the mother may develop a fever. Only when that has been going on for some time can bacteria enter and infect the breast.

So, try to drain the overfilled area of the gland frequently. (On the other hand, there's no need to empty your breasts *completely* each time.) Remember to let the let-down reflex work for you, and make sure that the baby opens his or her mouth wide and latches on correctly. During the feeding, gently massage the milk in the sore area forward toward the nipple. You can also massage like this when using a breast pump.

WILL BREAST-FEEDING CHANGE MY FIGURE?

Breast-feeding uses stored fats to produce milk. Prolonged breast-feeding may reduce the fatty layers on your hips and thighs, where fat built up during pregnancy. If you don't breast-feed, the fat is hard to get rid of by dieting, probably because nature has created it as a "reserve" for breast-feeding.

The breasts change in varying degrees for all women who have gone through a pregnancy. What probably changes them most is overfilling during the first few weeks after birth, when the connective tissues are more stretchable. Prolonged breast-feeding doesn't change the breasts more than short-term feeding. The best advice is to breast-feed frequently to avoid too much pressure in the breasts.

SMOKING

The nicotine in cigarettes *does* reach the baby through breast milk. So, if you quit smoking when you were pregnant, please don't start again. However, breast-feeding is so important

for mother and child that even smokers should breast-feed. Try to keep the number of cigarettes low, and don't smoke right before breast-feeding. Of course, protect your baby from inhaling any "second-hand smoke," too.

CONTRACEPTION

It is true that breast-feeding delays both <u>ovulation</u> (release of the egg) and <u>menstruation</u> (your "period"). That said, breast-feeding is *not* a reliable form of <u>contraception</u> (birth control). As long as your baby is being given *only* breast milk, and is nursing at night, it isn't likely that you will menstruate. However, you can conceive another child during the first ovulation after you give birth, which takes place sometime in the month *before* you start menstruating again. Out of 100 women who haven't started menstruating again yet, and who are not using any contraceptives, 2 will get pregnant again within 6 months of giving birth.

As soon as you start introducing mixed nutrition, the likelihood that you'll conceive again goes up. And, even if you haven't started menstruating in the second half of your baby's first year, the chances for getting pregnant again go up — to about 5 in 100 if you don't use birth control.

When you've started menstruating again, you *cannot* rely on breast-feeding to prevent new conception, no matter how short a time has lapsed since you gave birth.

If you want to use contraception, talk with your doctor or family planning clinic about the best methods for you. Condoms, diaphragms, and barrier methods are usually fine. If you want to use the pill, consult your doctor or family planning clinic about the best type to use while breast-feeding.

TIME OFF WORK TO BREAST-FEED

If you work outside the home, you may want or need to go back to work before you've finished breast-feeding. Check with your employer — usually the personnel department or benefits administrator is best — about whether they will allow you time off during the day to breast-feed (or use a breast pump). Perhaps you can arrange for "flex-time" in which you arrive early and/or stay late, taking some time off in the middle of the day. Company policies vary, and many small employers don't have a specific "breast-feeding policy," so you may need to negotiate.

BOTTLE-FEEDING

We know today that breast milk is best for babies. All warm-blooded animals make milk, but there are large differences between their milks. The fact that adult humans drink cow's milk, and produce formula based on cow's milk, doesn't necessarily mean that that's the best milk for humans — it's just easily available.

The first milk your breasts produce, colostrum, is full of important ingredients to nourish and protect your baby. So, even if you have decided to bottle-feed, it's good to give your baby these first important drops of milk.

CHOOSING A FORMULA

You should talk to your doctor or midwife about which formula is best suited to your baby. Your baby may not be able to digest some types of formula, but will thrive on others. It is normal to experiment with a few formulas before you find one that suits your baby.

Most formulas are based on cow's milk, so if your baby is allergic to cow's milk, you'll need to choose a soy formula. Fresh cow's milk should *not* be given to babies under 9 months to 1 year old.

If you want to make your own formula, here's one recipe (from the American Academy of Pediatrics) you might try:

- One 13-ounce can of evaporated milk (*not* condensed milk)
- 2 tablespoons (6 teaspoons) of light corn syrup or sugar (sucrose)
- 18 to 19 ounces of sterilized water (bottled or boiled)

Wash your hands and the top of the evaporated milk can with warm, soapy water. Open the can with a can opener that has been scalded with boiling water. Empty the can of evaporated milk into a sterilized (boiled) 1-quart jar with a screw-on top or airtight lid. Add the corn syrup or sugar. Fill the jar with sterilized water, which has been allowed to cool at room temperature (lukewarm if you're going to feed your baby right away). Close the jar tightly and shake it until the ingredients are thoroughly mixed together. Pour into baby bottles, and seal them with lids. Sterilize the bottles of formula by placing them upright in a pot of water and boiling the water for 25 minutes. Allow the formula in the bottles to cool before feeding your baby! Refrigerate any of the formula you don't use immediately. Use or throw out all of the formula within 24 hours.

If you make your own formula, follow the instruction exactly. Also, be sure that your doctor knows that you're using homemade formula, so that the necessary vitamin and mineral supplements (such as vitamin C and iron) can be given. Proper nutrition is needed for normal growth and development.

WHAT EQUIPMENT WILL I NEED?

If you decide to use traditional baby bottles, you'll need bottles and nipples, plus equipment to sterilize them. Alternatively, there are disposable bottle liners, so that you don't have to sterilize the bottles. You'll see a lot to choose from on the market, but the nipples that look and feel most like the breast are probably the best. The other thing to look out for is the size of the holes in the nipple. They should not be too small, because the baby could grow tired of sucking and swallow a lot of air. If the holes are too big, the baby will drink too fast and may have problems digesting. When you hold the bottle upside down, a steady stream of drops of formula should come out.

When and how much should I feed the baby?

Today, most people believe it's best to feed the baby when he or she shows signs of hunger. (See Feeding "on demand," on pages 23 to 24, for more information.) Every baby is different, but in the beginning it's usually 5 to 10 feedings in 24 hours. Some babies stop wanting to feed at night early on. Others keep wanting it for a long time. Some babies eat a lot, while others seem to need less. Calories provide energy. In general, until the baby is 5 months old, he or she will need 55 calories a day for each pound of body weight. About 3 ounces of formula, per pound, per day contains that amount of calories. Remember, babies vary — yours may need more than this or less.

Breast pumps

Some mothers think they have to bottle-feed with formula because they're returning to work. This isn't necessarily true. You can breast-feed all through your maternity leave if you work outside the home, even if it's just for a few weeks. With careful planning, you can use a breast pump to express your own milk, which you then store in the freezer. Or, if you are not able to do this, you can have your baby on formula during the day and breast-feed before and after. Remember, though: The baby needs to suck — or you need to express — breast milk at least once a day to keep producing it. Many women keep breast-feeding once or twice a day all through the first year, which will provide your baby with essential nutrients as well as forming a special bond. Ask your doctor, midwife, childbirth educator, or breast-feeding advisor for information about breast pumps.

CHAPTER 5

Nutrition for the Infant and Toddler

The foundation for healthful eating should be laid before the baby is born. Will you breast-feed or bottle-feed? How will you supplement — and then replace — breast milk or formula when the time comes? Children can breast-feed through the first year of life, but it's still a good idea to prepare a nutritional plan for infancy and toddlerhood.

You can get good nutritional advice from the doctor's office, clinic, hospital seminars, local health departments, or even some breast-feeding or childbirth groups. In recent years, experts have learned a lot about nutrition, which has led to changes in some dietary recommendations. Try to follow their guidelines, but know that you'll be tailoring any diet to fulfill your own baby's needs. Plus, your child's needs will change as he or she grows.

To make sure your child doesn't get malnourished, your nutritional plan should be well balanced. The diet should be varied. And, it should supply both nutrients and energy, to help ensure good growth and good health. Too little food will lead to slow growth. Foods have to supply enough calories (energy) to keep the body working and bones and muscles growing, in addition to those calories needed to provide energy to move around and play. But don't overdo it on the calories, either!

When planning your child's diet, remember that babies need lots of fluids (liquids), too.

PROTEINS

There's a great deal of difference among the proteins found in breast milk, cow's milk, and formula. Mother's milk is the only milk that contains human proteins, in the right amount for human babies. A major nutritional problem we have in the "industrialized" world is too *much* protein. This is especially problematic for children. High protein intake can be a burden on a baby's kidneys, especially if the baby isn't getting enough fluids. Formulas and cow's milk contain more proteins than mother's milk.

SUGARS

It's easy to forget that many foods contain "hidden sugars," especially in juice drinks, jellies, sweetened cereals, and some milk products. These sugars are "empty calories" that give a burst of energy but not much more. Eating a lot of sugar interferes with the absorption of iron and can damage the teeth.

FATS

Polyunsaturated fats and fatty acids help the brain develop and function. Using cod-liver oil (which also contains vitamins A and D) and vegetable oils will supply most of the crucial fatty acids. The omega-3 fatty acids are especially important. They aren't found in formulas, but can be found in mother's milk, oily fish (like tuna, sardines, herring, mackerel, salmon), and some oils. Ask the doctor's office about vitamin D supplements.

Even after weaning, your baby will need more fats than you do, relatively speaking. Whole milk, some food oils, and vegetable margarine can help you give your baby nutrition without resorting to "junk food."

FIBER

Plants — such as raw vegetables and corn — are the most important source of dietary fiber. Fiber helps prevent and treat constipation, by "moving things through" the digestive system. It's good to include some fiber-rich foods in your baby's diet, but not too much. If there's too much fiber, the baby will get full before he or she has received enough nutrients. Balance and moderation are key.

VITAMINS

Babies need a lot of vitamins during infancy to stay healthy, especially vitamins A, C, and D.

Even mother's milk doesn't contain enough vitamin D for most babies. And, our bodies can store only small amounts of vitamin D. Children need to get enough vitamin D during the first year of life, and all through childhood. This is especially important in the winter, in cold climates. Fortunately, most cow's milk and many cereals have been "fortified" with extra vitamin D. This helps prevent vitamin D deficiency, or rickets.

Vitamin A is found in most types of milk. Foods high in vitamin D probably also contain vitamin A. Carrots and tomatoes are important sources of vitamin A. Getting enough vitamin A helps prevent eye problems.

The B vitamins are a group of vitamins that are important for the body's metabolism.

We receive vitamin B through milk, grain products, and fortified cereals.

Vitamin C improves the absorption of iron from formula and grain products, among other things. Breast milk supplies enough vitamin C, if the mother maintains a healthful diet. Adding extra vitamin C to your diet won't add much vitamin C to your breast milk, but it won't hurt, either. Citrus fruit juices (orange, grapefruit, lemon, lime) are good sources of vitamin C.

IRON

Iron is used in the making of red blood cells and in some metabolic processes. The red blood cells help oxygen get to all of the tissues in our bodies. During the last part of pregnancy, your baby built up a "reserve" of iron from you. This stored iron is used until the baby starts receiving iron from other sources.

About half of the iron in the breast milk is absorbed. When weaning has begun, the baby's ability to absorb iron from the mother's milk will decrease. This is one of the good reasons to wait to introduce solid foods until the baby is 6 months old. Citrus fruits and baby cereal enriched with iron and vitamin C are important sources of iron from the second year of life on. Iron from table food will provide only about 10% of a child's daily need, but iron-enriched cereal will provide around 90%.

FLUORIDE

Fluoride is built into the enamel, or hard outer part, of the teeth when they are forming. So, children need to get fluoride to get strong teeth. Fluorinated water (found in many water supply systems), fluoride toothpaste, or fluoride supplements reduce the danger of tooth decay, slow the development of cavities, and even help repair minor tooth damage. Beware of giving your child too much fluoride in his or her diet, though.

DIETARY ADVICE FOR GOOD WEIGHT GAIN

The diet of infants and toddlers has to be adjusted to the child's age. During the early period, breast milk or formula provides all the nutrition. During the second half of the first year, grain-based baby cereal becomes important. Then what should follow is a mixed balanced diet. Good, steady weight gain and a happy baby are the best indicators of healthful development and well-being. Weight gain is largest during the first year of life.

"Normal" weight gain (approximate weights):
- 0–3 months: 7 ounces a week (in the range of 5 to 8 ounces)
- 3–6 months: 5 ounces a week (3-1/2 to 6 ounces)
- 6–9 months: 3-1/2 ounces a week (2-1/2 to 4-1/2 ounces)

9–12 months: 1-1/2 to 2-1/2 ounces
   a week
1–2 years: 4-1/2 to 5-1/2 pounds a year
2–5 years: 4-1/2 pounds a year

As the child grows and develops, there will be different demands and expectations about food. Learning healthful habits is important. However, children have different personalities and tastes, just like grown-ups. Infants may have periods of slow weight gain, even if they are eating well and acting happy. Know that this is normal.

OVERWEIGHT?

Weight should always be measured relative to height. As long as a baby's diet mainly consists of breast milk, he or she is not thought of as overweight, even if the weight is at the top of the weight charts. Infants who are being breast-fed shouldn't go on weight-reduction diets.

If your doctor says your child is overweight, it's important to look at what's being eaten. Try making a detailed "daily intake" list of exactly what your child is eating — the types of foods, quantities (by volume or weight), and times of the day or night when they are eaten. Until you do that, it might seem as though your child is not eating enough. Then you can look at what can be changed.

UNDERWEIGHT?

Remember that it's important to measure weight compared to height. A child is considered underweight if his or her weight is less than the weight of *three-quarters* of the other children his or her age and height.

Sometimes, a breast-fed or bottle-fed child is getting too little nutrition, even when he or she seems satisfied. If the child is being given additional food, do an accurate analysis of the diet, to see whether he or she is receiving enough nutrients. At the same time, you have to look at how often the child has bowel movements, and what they look and smell like.

GENERAL GUIDELINES FOR INFANT NUTRITION
Younger than 6 months
Breast milk (or formula) is the most important source of nutrition for young infants. As long as your baby is happy and healthy, gains enough weight, and has a normal sleep pattern, there's no reason to introduce other types of food.

If, however, the baby seems extremely hungry, sleeps only a little, and demands several meals during the night, you may need to supplement the breast milk or formula before he or she reaches 6 months of age. But first, try to increase your production of breast-milk, if you're breast-feeding.

It's important to remember that crying does not always mean hunger. One study of healthy babies showed that the children under 3 months of age cried for an hour and a half each day, and those between 3 and 5 months of age cried for an hour and 20 minutes! The children in the study had 5 periods a day with prolonged spells of crying!

You can start "mixed nutrition" by giving a few teaspoons of baby cereal at an evening feeding. Prepare the dry cereal with water or expressed breast milk.

FROM 6 TO 12 MONTHS OLD

When your child turns 5 or 6 months old, breast milk or formula alone may not provide enough nutrients or calories anymore. At that point, it's time to start supplementing the diet with solid foods, in the form of baby cereal and dinners. You'll probably start with cereals, then gradually add breads, fruits, vegetables, and other foods. As soon as the child has been introduced to solid foods, be sure to limit the amount of formula to 20 ounces a day! He or she can be given water for extra fluid.

The child should learn that foods have different tastes and consistencies. Meals at this stage are educational experiences. Hold off on foods that most often trigger allergies (such as fish, eggs, pies, beans, tomatoes, strawberries, and citrus fruits). This is especially important in families who already suffer from allergies. Prepared baby food is convenient but expensive. You can mash your own food or use a blender.

OLDER THAN 1 YEAR

Now's the time to build on the habits your child learned in the first year. Your child is being weaned and is getting more sociable. It is important to have at least one meal where the family is gathered together at a specific time. The meal should also be planned so that everyone is eating at least some of the same foods. Generally, you shouldn't try to force a child to eat. You can decide what the baby eats, but he or she should decide how much.

A child's stomach capacity is limited. If the food isn't nutritious enough, or if it has too much fiber, they can't eat enough to meet their large energy (calorie) needs.

If your child drinks a lot of cow's milk, it may be at the expense of other types of food, and the diet won't be varied enough. Whole milk gives a lot of energy from animal fat, but few nutritional substances like iron and vitamins A and D. If the iron is gotten from cereal and bread, and you use vegetable margarine or vegetable oils in meals that also contain some fat, low-fat milk can be substituted for whole milk. (Skim milk should not be offered until the child is 2 years old.) The key is balanced total nutrition.

WEANING

There is no set time for when a child should be weaned from breast milk or formula. Each mother will have to decide when she and her baby are ready. It's recommended that most children breast-feed for at least 1 year, or longer if possible.

WHOLE, LOW-FAT, AND SKIM MILK

Even when babies are fully weaned from breast milk, they shouldn't get too much cow's milk. Drinking too much cow's milk makes them feel full, but they probably won't be able to absorb enough iron.

The use of whole milk and other cow's milk products becomes an alternative at around 1 year of age, or later if you're still breast-feeding. Cow's milk should not be introduced until then. Recent studies indicate that early use of cow's milk can cause minor bleeding in the stomach and gut, and can lead to loss of iron (anemia). Cow's milk can also provide too-high levels of proteins and salts. And, some children are allergic to cow's milk. It's better to use a formula that is not based on cow's milk.

After 1 year, it's okay to gradually add whole milk. Fats are important for the development of the brain, and low-fat milk (1% or 2% fat) or skim milk (no fat) alone probably won't provide enough fat in the first 2 years. By using vegetable oils and vegetable margarine as substitutes for the fat in whole milk — on whole-grain foods and vegetables — the child will receive more of the "good" polyunsaturated fats in the diet.

CORN PRODUCTS

Corn products have a high calorie content. With breast milk or formula, corn products form a complete and balanced diet for the infant. It is natural to start with rice and corn when the child is being introduced to baby cereal. Wheat and oat flours, which contain <u>gluten</u>, can be given during the breast-feeding period, too.

MEAL-TIME

Having the family gather to eat meals together is a nice way to bond, to get to know each other's habits, and to introduce new foods to the baby. If schedules permit, try getting everyone together for one or more meals a day.

You don't need to buy ready-made baby food when your child is ready for foods other than breast milk or formula. If your own dinner is very spicy, chewy, or otherwise unsuitable, it may be fine to give the baby potatoes or vegetables mashed with a little sauce, margarine, or broth. Or, the baby can be given baby cereal or a slice of bread with a topping.

HOW MANY MEALS?

Babies will usually decide for themselves how many meals they should have. During the first few weeks, they'll usually adjust to 7 or 8 meals a day (every 3 hours), and later they'll want 5 or 6 meals (every 4 hours). Four meals a day are probably fine if the older baby is contented and eats well.

WHEN BABY IS SICK

Mother's milk is best for ill infants. But because infants are nose breathers, it may be hard for them to suck well when their nose is blocked. If that happens, you can try putting a few drops of salty water or special nose drops into your baby's nose before the feeding. If the baby can't suck, you should express milk from your breasts and give it with a bottle or a teaspoon. If he or she loses the appetite enough that your breasts start to over-fill, you'll have to express milk by hand or with a breast pump. That way, you'll keep producing milk — and you'll have extra breast milk in store for later use. Mother's milk can last for 2 to 3 days in the refrigerator, or about 6 months in the freezer.

If your child has <u>diarrhea</u> (loose bowel movements), he or she should stop drinking cow's milk. This does *not* apply to mother's milk; the child should continue to breast-feed. Mother's milk contains agents that protect the baby against infections and diarrhea. It's very important to give extra fluids, in the form of clear fluids, to children with diarrhea.

WHEN YOU ARE SICK

Good news... You don't have to stop breast-feeding if you aren't very ill. If you get a cold or mild virus, you should continue breast-feeding. Mother's milk contains antibodies that help protect the baby against infections.

If you get a fever, the amount of breast milk you produce might go down. In that case, try to breast-feed more frequently, even if you're tired. It's more important to spend your energy breast-feeding than doing chores. But if your own nutrition is suffering, be sure to call your doctor for advice. It's comforting to know that even if you're in the hospital, you *may* be able to breast-feed.

Be very cautious about taking medicines when you're sick. Ask your doctor, breast-feeding advisor, or pharmacist about which medicines will pass into your milk.

If you can't breast-feed for a few days, you can increase the milk production again by putting your baby to the breast more frequently, or try to maintain production by expressing the milk.

CHAPTER 6

Allergies

ALLERGY AND HYPERSENSITIVITY

Most people use the word "allergy" to describe all types of hypersensitivity. In this chapter, the most common forms of true allergy are described. A specific antibody — called IgE — is associated with these conditions. The IgE antibody is found in high levels in allergic people. It reacts with symptom-causing allergens such as pollen, mold spores, animal dander, dust mites, and certain types of food or medications.

Allergies can be triggered or worsened even by *non-allergic* factors such as infections or air-borne irritants. Plus, allergies give different symptoms to different children, and can range from mild to life-threatening. Therefore, allergies are difficult to classify, and prevention and treatment vary from child to child.

THE FETUS AND ALLERGY

IgE antibodies are formed in the third or fourth month of pregnancy. Nine out of 10 children with a high IgE count at birth later develop allergies. However, three-quarters of people with allergies had a normal IgE count at birth. Diets that avoid potential allergens such as eggs or cow's milk during pregnancy *do not* protect the unborn child from allergies. Therefore, you should eat normally (but well) when pregnant. On the other hand, smoking *does* appear to increase the risk of developing an allergy later on.

THE INFANT AND ALLERGY

Some newborns produce IgE antibodies soon after birth. These are primarily to proteins in foods such as eggs and cow's milk. Even the tiny amounts of such proteins present in breast milk are enough to trigger the process. Non-allergic children produce small amounts of IgE antibodies without having an allergic response. Some allergic children, however, produce high levels of IgE antibodies and develop allergic symptoms. Allergy to foods such as eggs, milk, and wheat may decline during toddler age, whereas allergy to fish, peas, peanuts, and shellfish lasts longer — perhaps throughout life.

ALLERGIC ILLNESSES DURING THE FIRST YEAR

Atopic eczema is common in the first year. The child first develops dry, rough, slightly itchy skin. This is followed by a rash that appears first on the face, then gradually spreads over large areas of the body. The rash may ooze and be crusty. It later moves to the back of the knees and inside the elbows. Much of the eczema during the first 12 months is related to food allergies, most commonly to eggs and cow's milk. Food allergies can also give other symptoms, such as vomiting, flushed skin, itchiness, hives, or allergic swelling (particularly around the mouth and eyes). Other, less common symptoms are diarrhea, difficulty breathing, or slow growth.

Respiratory symptoms may show up within the first month of life, but normally they don't appear until later in the first year. Early symptoms are a runny or blocked nose, sneezing, coughing, tendency to ear–nose–throat infections and bronchitis or bronchiolitis. More rare during the first year are allergic eye symptoms and runny nose. Take great care with these respiratory responses. If they aren't understood and attended to quickly, they can later develop into allergic asthma.

Allergic children may also have a sensitive digestive system, with tendency to colic, vomiting, frequent loose stools, and slow weight gain. Such children often have hypersensitive skin, respiratory system, and intestines before they develop an allergic illness. Fortunately, many hypersensitive children don't become allergic later on. Real food allergies are uncommon, but the risk of developing diet-related allergies is greater with infants than with toddlers. The intestinal system isn't fully developed in very young children, which can cause problems if the child receives sensitizing proteins (such as eggs or cow's milk) too early.

INHERITANCE AND ENVIRONMENT

The likelihood of developing allergies is about 6 in 10 if both parents are allergic, and 3 in 10 if only one parent is allergic. If neither parents has allergies, there is still a 1 in 10 chance that the child will develop some form of allergy. It's now accepted that we only inherit the *tendency* for allergy — not a particular allergic illness.

Factors in the environment can be divided into two groups. The first group consists of true allergens such as eggs, fish and seafood, dairy products, various grasses and tree pollens, dust, mold and fungal spores, feathers, and animal dander. These true allergens produce an IgE-type reaction and symptoms appear upon exposure. Other environmental factors that activate or aggravate allergic reactions can be considered a second group. These factors include air pollution, unhealthy indoor climate (including smoking), changes in diet, and so forth. This may explain why allergic diseases have increased so dramatically over the last decade or so.

BREAST-FEEDING AND ALLERGY

While breast-feeding, should you avoid eggs, cow's milk, etc. if your family has allergies? Research shows that eliminating such foods will reduce the levels of IgE antibodies and the symptoms of atopic eczema. But in the long run, there's no difference in frequency or severity of allergic illnesses. The most important thing is for you to eat a well-balanced diet. On the other hand, if your child develops atopic eczema or allergy during the breast-feeding period, you may want to try changing your diet.

When it's time to introduce other foods, you should wait until your child is a year old before introducing eggs, fish, peas, citrus fruits, and nuts if he or she — or close family members — are allergic.

PREVENTIVE ENVIRONMENTAL MEASURES

Infants are particularly vulnerable to developing allergies during the first few months of life. A healthy indoor climate is important for an infant disposed to allergy. If possible, avoid keeping animals and caged birds. This may be difficult to do if you already have a pet. Don't use bedding made of feathers or down. Even more importantly, avoid all smoking, both indoors and in the car. Cigarette smoke increases the frequency of allergy, bronchitis, and asthma.

Indoor air often contains *several hundred times* the amounts of polluting gases and particles than outdoor air. These pollutants are from building materials, furniture, cleaning products, etc. In recent years houses have become "tighter." The air is exchanged and replaced much more slowly, which contributes to indoor pollution.

Try to use wooden or linoleum-covered floors with loose, washable rugs in the rooms where your child sleeps and plays the most. If the floor is carpeted, it should be vacuumed frequently, at a time when the child isn't in the room. The carpet should be thoroughly shampooed or steam-cleaned twice a year. These rooms should be easily maintained and kept free from dust. Avoid dust-collecting curtains, wallpapers, toys, upholstered furniture, mattresses, and closets full of stored clothes. The bedding should be aired and washed regularly. Change the air in the room by opening all the windows for short periods of time (again when the baby isn't there). If there are pets in the home, they shouldn't be kept in the child's room.

Reducing irritants throughout the home is also important, but should be done within reason. Avoid using paint, varnish, perfume, insecticides, hair sprays, deodorants, cleaning liquids, waxes, and glue near children, and be particularly aware of indoor climate problems when redecorating the house.

Outdoor air is much cleaner than indoor air. It is, however, better to air the house from a side that has minimum exposure to outdoor pollutants such as car traffic, factories, or known sources of allergy such as pollinating trees.

Despite the fact that about 20% of all children develop some form of allergic reaction at least once in their life, the condition is mild or moderate for most of them. There is no need for thorough and expensive preventive measures until serious problems arise.

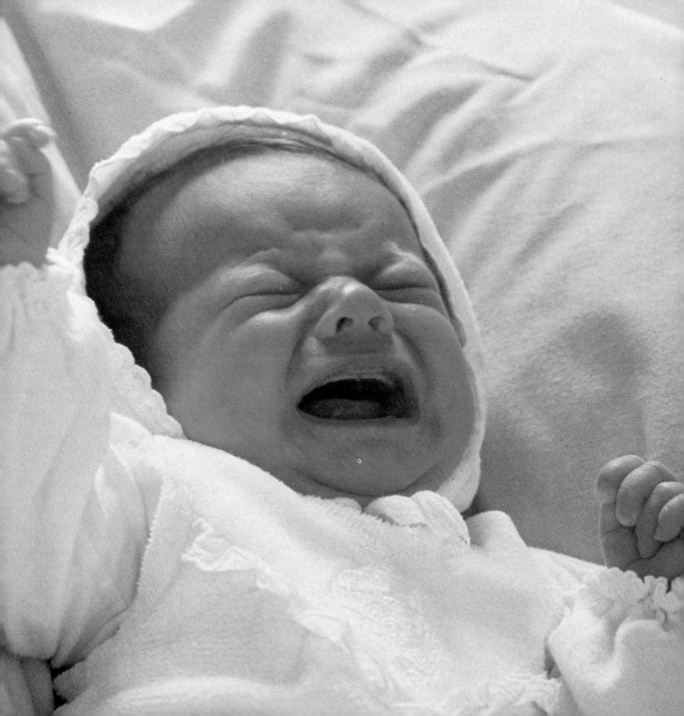

CHAPTER 7

Colic

WHAT IS COLIC?

All babies cry, usually 1 or 2 hours a day. It's their way of telling you that they're wet, hungry, tired, in pain, or lonely... But some babies cry a lot more than others. If a baby cries for *more than 3 hours a day, at least 3 days a week*, it's called <u>colic</u>.

Colic is quite common, appearing in up to 1 out of 3 infants. It usually starts when the baby is between 2 and 4 weeks old, and usually disappears at around 3 months of age. The symptoms can vary in how intense and how frequent they are. A child suffering from colic is usually healthy, feeds eagerly, has a good appetite, and looks completely fine when not crying.

Colic shows up as bouts of irritability with crying. It's more common in the afternoon, evening, and night-time hours, so the baby being tired may play a part. None of the usual methods to calm a baby seems to work — neither feeding, nor holding, nor rocking stops the crying.

A typical crying spell usually lasts 4 or 5 minutes. When it's over, the baby relaxes a little, and is just about to fall asleep when the next spell starts. You can often hear movement in the intestines and gases bubbling in the stomach. The concept of colic comes from the traditional view of the problem being caused by cramps in the digestive system.

WHAT CAUSES COLIC?

The cause of a baby's colic is very hard to figure out. According to international studies, bottle-fed children are just as likely to develop colic as breast-fed children. Some researchers have found that colic is more common in industrialized countries like ours. Colic is more common in first-born children. There may be a connection between colic and difficult birth. And, stress and isolation might play a role.

Another possible cause of colic is if the baby's stomach and intestines trap extra air that was sucked in while feeding, and the baby isn't able to burp during or after the meal.

Swedish researchers have discovered that cow's milk sometimes affects colic, too. Their studies showed that cow's milk contains substances that can cause colic. If a breast-feeding mother is eating or drinking any dairy products (milk, cheese, butter, ice cream, etc.) these substances might be transferred to the baby.

AVOIDING DAIRY PRODUCTS

Because a breast-feeding mother's consumption of dairy products may contribute to her baby's colic symptoms, a first step might be to stay away from all dairy products for 3 or 4 days. This relieves the problem in about 1 out of 5 colicky babies. If avoiding dairy products works, keep doing this. But be sure that you receive enough calcium — calcium supplements can help.

If you're bottle-feeding, find out what's in the formula. Some formulas are based on cow's milk; they are particularly likely to cause colic in some babies. Experimenting with different formulas may help solve the problem.

PREVENTING TRAPPED AIR

Try reducing the amount of air your child is swallowing by becoming aware of what's going on at meal-time. Does the baby suck very vigorously? Is it easier to burp him or her if you take small breaks in the feeding? Is it better to lay the baby on his or her tummy after the meal, perhaps with the main part of the body slightly elevated? Are the holes in the baby bottle's nipple too small or too big? Are there other things in the diet or environment that could contribute to the unrest?

PEACE AND SECURITY

Parents worry when their baby cries and they're unable to comfort the child. The baby might sense that worry, and react by crying even more. Plus, when crying, the baby usually swallows air again, and the vicious circle continues.

Mother and child are so "in tune" with each other that they can be very sensitive to stress and other tensions in their environment. It is, therefore, important to try to stay calm in this stressful situation. The crying spells probably don't mean that there's anything seriously wrong with the baby or with you as a parent. But if the doctor hasn't already confirmed that your baby has colic, make sure you check with the doctor first, to make sure that nothing more serious is going on.

Some colicky children do better in peaceful surroundings. You might try limiting the amount of loud noise, number of visitors, and other forms of stimulation, particularly during feedings. Look at the baby and talk to him or her in soothing, loving tones. Try a baby massage, gently patting and stroking your child. (See Chapter 8, "Baby Massage," pages 49 to 51.) During the crying spells, try putting on some soft, peaceful music that you liked to listen to when you were pregnant. Put the baby in your lap and gently, slowly rock in a rocking chair or hammock. Sometimes, these methods work quite well.

USING VIBRATIONS

Many parents have found that colicky babies are soothed when they're taken for a ride in the car (secured in a car seat, of course). You can use a ride to "test" if a baby rocker might help. An odd-sounding alternative is to put the baby in a car seat and place him or her on a running clothes dryer. If you do that, be absolutely sure that you keep a hand on the baby *at all times,* so he or she doesn't get vibrated off the dryer!

These methods use a combination of vibrations and continual sound that can distract the baby's attention from the discomfort colic brings. He or she may be able to recognize songs and music you played during the pregnancy. It's important to use these methods at an early stage, though. Their effect gradually wears off such that past 3 months of age, it's not likely that they'll help much anymore. Babies that age are less easily distracted, and they may have even learned to get some comfort from screaming.

STOP SMOKING

It has been proven that mothers who smoke are more likely to have colicky children than non-smoking mothers. If you — or others around the baby — smoke, see whether the colic improves if you stop.

MEDICINES AND HERBS

Some babies respond well to fennel or caraway tea. These herbs can be found in the seasonings section of the grocery store or health food store. Boil 1 teaspoon in 3-1/2 ounces of water for 2 minutes. Let the mixture steep for 2 more minutes. Then, strain with a strainer or some cheesecloth. Give 1 teaspoon to the child at each feeding. A doctor trained in homeopathy can prescribe a natural remedy that may help, too.

Some doctors recommend simethicone drops, which get rid of some of the intestinal gases. These drops work very well, and they usually have no side effects. Ask your doctor or the local pharmacist for some guidance. In more serious cases, the doctor may prescribe something stronger.

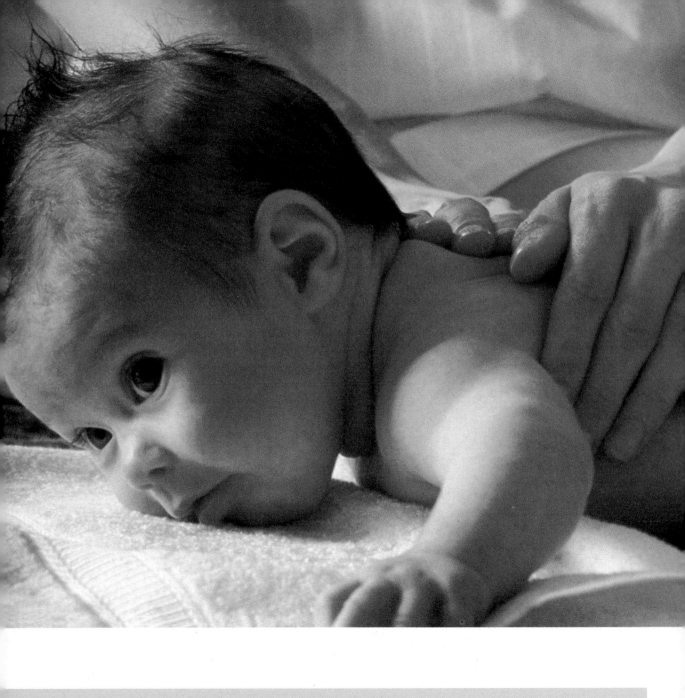

CHAPTER 8

Baby Massage

WHAT IS BABY MASSAGE?

Baby massage offers a unique way to communicate with your newborn, and in a way that he or she will recognize from the time in your uterus. Massage continues that intimate physical bond from when he or she was constantly massaged by the amniotic fluid. Soft, loving, rhythmic massage can help give the infant a secure and positive attitude to life outside the womb.

Most cultures have developed some form of baby massage. Mothers all over the world have intuitively understood the infant's need for touch and intimate physical contact. Baby massage is still widespread in countries like Russia and India. In some areas of India, the art of massage is being handed down from mother to daughter as a natural part of the art of caring for a child.

THE 3 BIGGEST ADVANTAGES OF BABY MASSAGE

1. Daily baby massage contributes to the development of a warm, intimate relationship between parents and child. Almost all of the elements of "parent bonding" are found in massage and can strengthen this important bond. Through massage, you become familiar with your child's "body language" and can closely follow his or her physical and psychological development. (See Chapters 12 and 13 for more about your child's development.)
2. Massage strengthens and regulates the circulation of the blood, breathing, and digestion. Gassy stomach is common in infants, and can often be released by a light "colic massage" (see below). Colic pains can be reduced, and often completely disappear, by regular massage.

3. Massage releases tensions. As a result of scientific research, we know today that infants are influenced by their mother's physical and emotional condition during the pregnancy. The birth itself can be a difficult process for the child. The transition to a new and unknown world isn't easy, either, and the amount of knowledge the baby must acquire during the first year can also be a strain. Through baby massage, both positive and negative experiences can be released. Stress may be expressed by being tearful and irritable. It can then be good to cry in a parent's arms, and a long nap often follows.

Baby massage isn't difficult to do, and some groups arrange classes for parents and infants. Learning baby massage through books — especially books with pictures — is still the easiest alternative for many people.

HOW TO GIVE THE MASSAGE

Baby massage can be started right after birth. A massage should be enjoyed, and not forced upon the baby.

Choose a warm room where the temperature is at least 75°F, and where you and your baby won't be disturbed. Put the baby in front of you, either on the bed, on a table, or on a mat on the floor. Make sure you are sitting comfortably, and try to relax before you start. Talk to your baby about the massage.

Use a natural oil (such as almond or olive) or a lubricating cream to make your fingers glide over the baby's body without pulling his or her skin. *Don't* use adult massage oils, which can irritate a baby's skin. Put a little of the oil or cream into the palm of your hand until it's warm.

The massage can now begin. Be gentle and pay attention to how your baby responds to your touch.

CHAPTER 9

Baby Care

First-time parents often feel insecure about how to handle and care for their newborn baby. The doctor's office, midwife, or maternity ward can give you sound advice and provide you with initial experience in caring for the little one. Do talk to them if you have *any* questions about baby care. You may also wish to join a local parents' group.

In most birthing centers and in some hospitals, your baby will be allowed to stay with you at all times. This is a good way for you to start to get to know each other. Encourage your partner to spend time with the two of you, also, in the first hours and days.

If you're a single mother or working mother, be assured that you can do a great job of caring for your baby! Make sure that you take good care of yourself — and your baby — by getting enough rest and by accepting offers of help from family, friends, and support groups.

BATHING

Most infants love to be bathed. Perhaps that's because their skin was wet for 9 months when they were in the womb. If you talk to your baby when you bathe him or her, you'll receive eye contact and smiles back. And yes, infants *do* smile — it's not just gas! Most babies get sleepy after a bath.

Your baby can probably be bathed soon after birth, regardless of whether the umbilical cord stump has fallen off. If the baby's skin isn't too dry, he or she can have a bath every day or two. However, if the skin is dry, it's best to not bathe your baby too frequently.

The room where the baby is being bathed should be comfortably warm (about 72°F). The bath water itself should be between 93°F and 99°F. If the water is warmer or colder, your baby may be afraid of the next bath.

Use a small plastic tub to help your baby feel more secure. Have a large towel ready to wrap the baby in after the bath, plus diaper and clothes. Use mild, fragrance-free soap *in* the water, but don't apply soap directly onto the baby. Ease the baby slowly into the water and give him or her time to adjust. Keep a gentle but tight grip around your baby's armpit and then slide your hand toward the bottom of the tub. Put your hand under the baby's neck and wash him or her with your other hand. This will provide enough support for the baby and will prevent your arm from getting tired.

Use a soft face cloth and start by washing the face and the hair, then do the same with the rest of the body.

Wash the <u>genital area</u> carefully. Be especially careful not to rub girls too hard, as the skin down there is delicate and gets sore easily. Wash from the front to the back, so that bacteria from the bowel won't get into the urinary tract and cause infection. With baby boys, it isn't necessary to pull back the foreskin of the penis. If your baby boy has been <u>circumcised</u>, don't tub bathe him until the area of circumcision is dry.

Remember to dry well behind the ears; otherwise the area may become sore. Don't use creams or talcum powder. A little <u>corn starch powder</u> can be used in the crease of the baby's neck, in the armpits, and around the groin. Allow your baby to lie and kick without the restraints of clothes — most babies love it! If his or her bottom is a little sore, let it "air" for a while after each bath and diaper change.

Is there anything more lovely than the smell of a freshly bathed infant? Make this time something you both look forward to. Take your time bathing your child. You — *and* the baby and the rest of the family — are all learning what works best for all of you. Why not take the opportunity and give the baby a massage. Use a little oil (such as almond oil) after the bath and massage the whole body gently. The baby enjoys being handled, and often you will have wonderful closeness during these moments! (For more information about massages, turn to Chapter 8, on pages 49 to 51.

CARING FOR THE BELLY BUTTON

The umbilical cord is usually cut at birth, and a clip or elastic band is attached near the baby's tummy to prevent the blood vessels in the <u>navel</u> (belly button) from rupturing. The cord stump will shrink and eventually fall off, often before you and the baby leave the maternity ward. However, even before the stump falls off, your baby can be bathed. The belly button sometimes oozes a little clear fluid, or some blood may trickle out. Use a cotton swab to clean it.

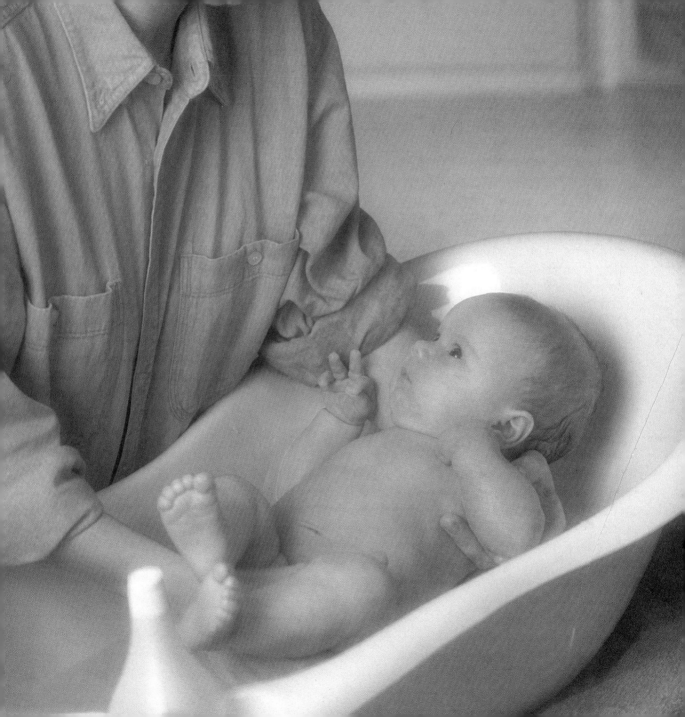

CHANGING THE BABY'S DIAPER

Preparing

Take all the time you need to change your baby. He or she will need to be changed 5 or 6 times a day in the early going, so you'll be getting a lot of practice! Infants like to be picked up and cared for, so make changings a time of enjoyment for both of you...You can use them to have nice little interactions. Remember, that's far more important than whether the diaper is perfectly done!

The surface you change the baby on should be soft. You needn't invest in a separate changing table (though they are convenient). You can use a table or low dresser instead, with a changing mattresses on top of it. Put a towel on the changing table or changing mattress, to make it even softer and easier to clean up. If your changing table has a strap, don't use it.

Arrange the changing area so that everything you'll need is in easy reach. This includes the diapers and any clothes you're going to dress the baby in. Have a basket with these and other items right at your fingertips:

- pre-moistened baby wipes, or mild liquid soap and a damp wash-cloth
- baby lotion or baby oil
- moisture-barrier creams and corn starch powders
- cotton balls
- cotton swabs

It's very important to wash your hands before changing the baby.

Never leave an infant on the changing table, *not even for a moment!* If you have to interrupt a changing, put your baby back into the crib.

How to change a diaper

The diaper should be changed *every* time your baby has a bowel movement. If a baby is left in a dirty diaper for too long, the skin will get sore. Diapers will be wet frequently, however, since babies can't control their bladder. Change the diaper if it's *very wet;* if only damp it's not necessary to change it. Most breast-fed babies will both wet and soil their diapers, so it may be wise to change the baby *after* feedings. Save a little milk if your baby falls asleep more easily right after being fed.

Wash your baby's bottom while changing the diaper to remove any urine and bowel movements. After the washing, wrap your baby in a towel — babies love to have their bottoms "aired." You may wish to apply a moisture-barrier cream after each changing.

Disposable diapers, which come in a variety of sizes, are easy to put on and secure with adhesive strips on the side. If you use cloth diapers, they'll have to be folded on the top so that liquids don't leak out. With baby girls, you fold the diaper twice at the back, and with boys twice in the front. Then, turn the baby again and continue dressing him or her. You don't have to change the baby's clothes each time, unless they're wet or soiled.

Night changings

Most infants wake up at least once a night in need of being changed. It's often recommended that a baby try to regulate his or her own changing times, though that may be hard to achieve. But parents also need their rest if they are to provide for their baby's needs.

Try to adjust the baby's rhythm to also suit you. If, for instance, the evening changings take place just before midnight, you'll get into a very tiring pattern. It'd probably be better to start at about 9:00 PM, to let you get a little sleep before the next changing at about 2:00 AM or 3:00 AM. (There are large variations here.) Don't despair if your child doesn't quickly find a set rhythm. But if you're exhausted from getting up at night, maybe someone else in the family can take over so that you can get 1 or 2 full nights' sleep.

If you wish, the baby can sleep in a crib next to your bed or in your own bed. Most parents are insecure at the beginning, and tend to check on their baby frequently. It'll take a few weeks before you feel more confident.

Night changings should be a calm and quiet time, so avoid strong lighting and loud voices. The baby will gradually learn that night-time is sleep-time.

DRESSING THE BABY

Lay your baby on the back while you dress him or her. If you're using a tee-shirt under the other clothes, pull it gently over the baby's head. Put two of your fingers inside the sleeve. Take hold of the baby's hand and carefully pull it through. If you need to snap or fasten anything on the back, turn the baby over onto the tummy, but remember to *always* support the head. Practice makes perfect! Babies usually don't mind if you take your time changing and dressing them.

DIAPER RASH

It can get hot and moist under a diaper, especially during the night when a longer time may pass between changings. Urine and warm dampness can easily cause diaper rash, in which the skin becomes red and spotty.

If your child develops diaper rash, it is important to let him or her be without a diaper for a while after each changing and at bedtime. Let the baby lie naked on a clean cloth, and make sure clothing is loose enough. In addition, use a barrier cream on the rash before putting the diaper on. Persistent rash, especially when normal barrier creams fail to help, can cause fungal infections, which are harmless but should be treated according to advice from a doctor or other health professional.

RASHES AND DRY SKIN

During the first few weeks of life, many babies develop a red, spotty rash on the skin. It usually appears as blotches, mainly on the face. This "heat rash" is quite harmless, and causes the baby little or no discomfort. Check to see if the baby is too hot, and adjust the clothing accordingly. You can also use some baby skin cream to keep the skin soft and smooth.

Infant skin is often dry, and may peel a little during the first few weeks. Although this isn't dangerous, peeling skin can benefit from a little skin cream or baby lotion.

Many children develop red spots with a little white center. These spots are quite normal, and don't require treatment. If, however, your baby has blisters that produce pus, contact the doctor.

A lot of infants develop a crusty scab on their scalp. This is called cradle cap. If it covers a large area, you can rub the scalp with a little oil (such as almond oil) at night and wash it gently away the next morning. If your child has hair, you can use a good comb to try to carefully remove some of the cradle cap from the head. Cradle cap disappears on its own without treatment, with no discomfort to the baby.

SLEEP

Right after you bring home your newborn is a time for "getting to know each other." It's not easy for either of you to settle into a clear sleep pattern, and you may wonder whether your baby is particularly restless.

Babies are little individuals in many ways, including their sleep patterns. Some children sleep a lot, and others sleep less. At about 6 weeks, you'll begin to notice that your baby wakes up not only when hungry, but also when rested and ready to participate in what's going on.

Some mothers notice that their baby wakes up both in the afternoon and in the evening. That can be tiring, especially if the baby refuses to calm down after being fed or played with. Perhaps a stroll outside in fresh air may help, or some massage to ease tummy ache. (See Chapter 8, "Baby Massage," pages 49 to 51.) This problem eventually disappears after a few weeks. However, if you are exhausted and concerned that something might be wrong with the baby, do call your doctor.

CRYING

You will learn to interpret your baby's cries after a while. You'll understand when he or she is hungry, or in pain, or wants attention. Most parents will immediately react by trying to comfort their child and find out what's causing the crying. They'll pick up the baby, cuddle and rock him or her, or carry the baby around. Minutes seem to pass very slowly if the child continues to cry. If you feel unsure of what to do, talk with friends and relatives who have children. Experiment with the different advice you receive, and perhaps you'll find some tips that help. The doctor's office or a parent's support group can be useful here.

FRESH AIR

Infants like to lie outside in fresh air. If the temperature is warm enough — but not too hot — newborns even can nap outside. Use common sense and your own judgment as to whether it's too cold out. Shield the baby carriage from wind, and never let it out of your sight! In hot weather, place your baby in the shade, away from direct sunlight. Also remember to keep a thin net over the baby carriage to keep insects out.

When the weather doesn't permit you to take your baby outside, you can leave him or her in front of an open window for a while. Remember to dress the baby well, and don't overdo. Usually you can dress a baby in one more layer than you are wearing.

INFANTS IN THE CAR

Many people wonder whether they can take a newborn for a trip in the car. The answer is yes, if you're prepared. In the winter, make sure the car is warmed up first, and dress the baby warmly. During the summer, it's extremely important to remember to *never ever* leave a child alone in the car. Temperatures quickly rise to dangerously high levels, and other things can happen.

Remember to bring a diaper change for any outings. For longer journeys, incorporate frequent stops into the plan, for everyone's sake. Take along a food cooler to store your child's formula, drinks, and food. And remember, smoking and children in the car don't go together!

Car seats and seat belts save lives! Always use a car seat for children up to age 4 or 40 pounds. After that, children — and adults — should *always* wear seat belts. For information about securing children in the car, see pages 119 to 120.

BABY SWIMMING

Baby swimming is popular, and courses are taught at many swimming pools and clubs. There are often long waiting lists, so it may be a good idea to put your name down soon after the birth.

CHAPTER 10

Baby Clothes and Equipment

In this chapter, you'll find some suggestions for clothes and equipment your baby may need. You might want to wait a little while to see what you really need as time goes on. Friends, relatives, and others will often give or lend you clothes and equipment. You needn't buy everything new. And remember, the most important things are free: your attention, your time, and your love.

THE BASIC WARDROBE

This is an "ideal" list — you can definitely manage with less. It's more important for clothes to be clean and to fit than for them to be brand new.

Baby clothes should be soft and loose. Underwear should be made of cotton and able to withstand being boiled. Infants don't like having things pulled over their head, so use open vests and cardigan sweaters, rather than pull-overs. It may be a good idea to wait to see

Stretch suits	4–6
Shirts or vests	6–8
Pants	2–3
Baby gowns	4–6
All-in-one padded suits	1–2
Coats & jackets	1–2
Cardigan sweaters	2–3
Hats & bonnets	2–3
Cotton receiving blankets	3–4
Cotton towels (large & small)	3–4

Diapers
 Disposable: 1 big box (about 60 per week)

 Cloth: 3–4 dozen cloth (twice that for diaper service), plus liners and covers, large safety pins, diaper pail

PLUS:
Cotton balls, cotton swabs, pre-moistened wipes, moisture-barrier cream, oils, corn starch powder

the size of your baby before buying the smallest infant clothes. Some babies will have outgrown them at birth, while others "swim" in them.

Infants like to have something soft around them for the first couple of months. Wrap your baby in a blanket, and let him or her wear a little hat made out of cotton or silk.

BEDDING

You may be using a bassinet or crib. These items are often passed down in families, which can be a nice way to keep traditions alive. However, you should probably browse in baby furniture stores anyway, to see whether what you have meets current safety guidelines. For example, the bars in a crib should be spaced closely enough (less than 2 and 3/8 inches apart).

Cover the insides of the bassinet or crib with bumpers. The mattress must be firm and shouldn't be too thin. If it's covered in plastic, it may be a good idea to place a cotton towel under the sheet, to avoid dampness.

Do not use a pillow. For infants who like to rest their head on something soft, you can fold a small flannel cloth or something similar.

Many newborns have allergies or sensitivities, so quilts or comforters that aren't filled with feathers or down are best. Choose a lightweight one. There's a large variety of comforter covers; 2 or 3 are enough, plus 4 or 5 flannel or cotton sheets.

Key things to remember when you are looking for the first wardrobe are:

- The clothes should be soft and comfortable, and without any hard seams.

- They must be big enough for the baby to grow in.

- The shape must be practical and loose; babies need to be able to move freely.

- The clothes should be of good quality, durable, not shrinkable, and able to withstand high washing temperatures.

- Clothes next to the skin should be made of natural fibers such as cotton, silk, or wool.

- The material must be fire resistant.

CHANGING

A <u>changing table</u> is not entirely necessary, but it is practical and offers you a good working height as well as room to keep cleaning items and clothes. If you decide not to buy a changing table, there are very useful <u>changing mattresses</u> on the market, which can be put on top of any flat surface to create an excellent changing area.

A <u>baby bathtub</u> is useful, although you can also use the bathroom sink, at least in the beginning. Make sure the baby doesn't ever come near hot taps or sharp or breakable objects! The bath should be a nice time for both of you. A couple of new, soft <u>bath towels</u> may be good to invest in. A bunch of thin, soft <u>washcloths</u> made of gauze are also useful.

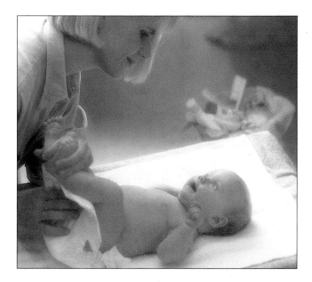

THE BABY CARRIAGE OR STROLLER

The most important thing here is to check that the <u>baby carriage</u> or <u>stroller</u> is fire resistant and washable. The material should also be waterproof. Plus, it should have brakes on *both* sets of wheels, and attachments for harnesses. Make sure there is enough room inside for a comforter and maybe a blanket. Carriages and strollers with detachable baby carriers are useful.

Consider your needs before you purchase this item. How will you use it, where, and how frequently? If you are going to take it in and out of a car constantly, it should be light

and easy to fold, and not too big for your trunk. It isn't necessarily true that the best carriages and strollers are the most expensive ones...Fashion trends also affect the price tag. They can also be bought second hand (be sure to check them out carefully first). Buy one that satisfies *your* situation.

THE BABY CARRIER

A <u>baby carrier</u> that you strap onto the front or back of your body may be a good alternative or supplement to the carriage or stroller. The baby receives good body contact and gets to see more of his or her surroundings. Your child is always close to you and under your watchful eye, so he or she will feel safe. The baby is being stimulated by movements and visual images. A baby carrier is also practical; it is reasonably inexpensive and doesn't take a lot of space in the car or on the bus.

A baby can be carried this way from a few weeks of age, but it's important that the carrier support the back and neck. And, the carrier must also be comfortable to the people who wear it!

CAR SEATS

If you have a car, or will be in one with your child, a car seat for the child *isn't* a luxury — it's an absolute necessity! Many babies and young children die each year because they weren't in a car seat when an accident occurred. Make sure you get a federally approved car seat.

There are many car seats on the market, in a range of prices. Buying a car seat is only half the story. It's also essential that the seat be fitted correctly in your car. Read all the manufacturer's instructions! Remember, too, that not every seat fits every car. Try several and ask around before you get one. And, consult a consumer's bureau or a doctor's group.

Infant carriers are suitable for babies from birth to around 6 months of age, at which time you'll need a larger car seat that can be used until the child is about 4 years old. Infant carriers are useful because they are lightweight for lifting in and out of the car, you don't need to wake the baby, they're easy to carry, comfortable for newborns, and can double as a low seat or rocker at home. The major disadvantage is that you will have to buy another car seat in 6 to 9 months.

Combination seats are suitable from birth to around 4 years — rear facing for the first 9 months and then forward facing to the age of 4. The main advantage of these seats is that they will last you 4 years. The main disadvantage is that they are heavy and not designed to be moved — you may have to wake your baby when getting out, they may not be as cozy or comfortable as an infant carrier, and you'll have to buy another seat if you're planning to have another baby within 4 years.

Notes

CHAPTER 11

Baby Shoes

Baby feet! Aren't they beautiful? Imagine — within 18 months your child will walk on them! Small, active, and soft...For how long? Few babies are born with foot problems, but how many adults have soft, beautiful feet with no discomforts?

Children's feet are continually growing and developing, and the bones, joints, and tissues are very soft and flexible. This means that the feet are vulnerable. They can form in the wrong shape if subjected to too much pressure from tight body-suits, socks, and (especially) shoes.

Infant booties should be soft, flexible, warm, and loose-fitting.

The purpose of shoes is to protect the feet against cold, wet, and hard and sharp objects. Shoes should be considered *a protection when protection is needed*. The first baby shoes should be purchased when the baby is walking outdoors. Shoes don't have to be expensive — shop around.

The human foot has three parts that footwear needs to especially protect and support:

1. A rounded, soft, buffer of a heel at the back of the foot
2. A flexible but stable long arch under the foot
3. A strong, straight big toe, plus 4 flexible little toes

WHAT SHOULD I LOOK FOR WHEN CHOOSING SHOES?

Many parents choose shoes that are too hard or stiff for young feet. Contrary to popular belief, *freedom of movement* is much more important than support. Unless your child has a rare deformity of the feet, orthopedic shoes are not necessary and may even damage the feet. Good children's shoes should protect against damage and dirt, but don't have to provide sturdy support. The most important features of shoes intended for outdoor use and activities on a hard surface are the following:

- The shoe must be long enough, be wide enough, and support the back of the foot.
- The area around the heel should be molded and contain a shock-absorbing layer.
- The front part has to be wide enough that all of the toes can move freely. *The big toe must be able to point straight inside the shoe!* The shoes should be shaped such that when they are placed next to each other, there's no gap between them.
- The sole should be soft and flexible, to allow free movement of the heel and toes and development of the foot. You can test whether a shoe is flexible enough in the shoe store. Bend the shoe from toe to heel, then fold the shoe diagonally. If this is easy to do, the sole is flexible enough for young feet.

It is important that shoes "breathe." Shoes made of leather or canvas are best. Leather and canvas absorb some foot moisture and bring it to the surface, where it can evaporate. They can also adjust their shape to that of the foot. The shoe lining should be of leather, wool, or another natural fiber. Synthetic materials can be too airtight — foot sweat and fungus can be a problem even for small children.

Soles and heels should be made of a flexible, durable material such as rubber. They should be shaped to help the child to stand up well. To help avoid foot-twisting accidents, the shoes' heels shouldn't be too high.

The opening of the shoe must be flexible, to let you adjust the tightness of the fit. Lace-ups, Velcro® fasteners, or broad straps are best. Shoes with Velcro® fasteners are easy for a child to take on and off, which eases the dressing procedure and delights the child by enabling him or her to "do it myself!"

WHAT SIZE SHOES SHOULD I BUY?

Feet vary greatly, ranging from small and narrow, to long and wide, and they may have a low, medium, or high arch.

Shoe length

Have your child stand up when you measure the feet, so that the full body weight rests on the feet. Measure each foot from the tip of the big toe to the back of the heel. The shoes should be about 1/2 inch longer than the feet. This allows for growth of about 1/4 inch, plus another 1/4 inch or so of "slide length" that the toes need when walking. If shoes are longer than that, the feet will slide around and not be supported well enough. If shorter, there will be too much pressure on the toes.

Youngsters' feet grow rapidly, and you'll have to constantly check that your child's toes aren't touching the front of the shoe. Be aware that your child *won't* notice if the shoes do not fit. Because the feet are so soft and moldable, your child will feel no pain if shoes are too tight. The feet grow in spurts, on average about 1/2 inch a year during childhood, and about 1 inch during adolescence.

Shoe width

The general rule is that the inside of the shoe should be about 1/3 inch wider than the foot. Most shoe stores have a device designed to measure the foot accurately. The child stands on the device, and the salesperson pushes little sliders up against the foot to measure its length and width. Some companies make shoes in different widths, so you can find a shoe that really fits your child's foot. The most important thing in buying shoes is to make sure that the foot has enough room to grow and develop.

SHOES ARE NOT A NATURAL PART OF THE BODY

Your child should walk without shoes as often as possible...That is, indoors, and outdoors during nice weather. This allows the toes to move freely, the muscles to develop well, and the blood to circulate naturally. It also gives your child the opportunity to feel and experience the feet in a different way than when they're "wrapped up" in shoes.

CAN CHILDREN INHERIT SHOES?

This is *not* recommended, because a foot that has not yet finished developing can be damaged by wearing a shoe that's been shaped by another foot. Children's feet are very different, and shoes fit only the first owner.

MATCHING THE SHOES TO THE SITUATION

When you are buying shoes, think about when and where they'll be worn. Indoor shoes and summer shoes should be light and soft. Winter shoes should be thicker, but also light and soft. It's healthful — for the feet and for the shoes — that the shoes be changed according to need.

FOOT EXERCISES

Children make sure that their feet get a lot of exercise. Additional exercises are unnecessary, so long as the feet are given enough freedom of movement from infancy on.

Infants and toddlers move their feet as much as they move their hands. When a 5-month-old baby grabs an object with both hands, he or she grabs with the feet at the same time. Fingers are usually allowed to be free, whereas toes are often limited in socks, tights, or stretch suits. Let your baby lie without socks several times a day, and ensure that any foot coverings are loose and large enough for the whole foot, especially the toes.

Play with your child's feet. Let the baby grab your hand with the toes and enjoy the movements. When your child is older, it's important that rolling, crawling, walking, and running be allowed without socks or shoes.

CHAPTER 12

Physical Growth and Development

In the first year, children grow and develop more rapidly than at any other time of their life. Foundations for good health are built during this period. It is, therefore, very important that your baby be given a good start. This chapter addresses the physical, or bodily, development of the infant.

THE HEALTHY INFANT

Every newborn is different, in both physical appearance and temperament. The healthy infant is round and cuddly, does more smiling than crying, and gets more and more active and curious by the day.

Newborns are calm and contented when given food or when picked up and rocked. From the very start, humming and soft words seem relaxing. During this period, the baby sleeps most of the time. The most highly developed senses are taste, smell, and touch. A new baby has a number of primitive reflexes.

Activity is otherwise limited to sneezing and coughing, swallowing and eating.

WEIGHT AND LENGTH

A child can weigh quite a lot less than "average," be shorter than "average," and still be absolutely normal in every aspect.

The average weight for a child is about 7-1/2 pounds at birth, a little more for boys and a little less for girls. During the first 3 days, the baby will lose about 5 to 10 ounces. Don't worry, this is perfectly normal. The birth weight will be gained back within 1 or 2 weeks. The weight doubles over the first 5 months, and triples by age 1. Babies gain the most weight in the beginning, particularly if they were premature or of low birth weight.

The average length of a baby at birth is between 18 and 21 inches. After 2 months the length is about 22-1/2 inches, after 4 months about 25 inches, and at 1 year about 30 inches.

Good indication that a baby is healthy is a smooth growth curve, with length increasing along with weight. But, "smooth" doesn't necessarily mean "constant"...Your child will probably go through a number of growth spurts and slow-growth periods, too. Try not to compare your own child's growth pattern too closely with other children's. There are always individual differences, and genetics plays an important role, too. Of far greater importance than weight and length is the baby's well-being — that he or she is healthy, energetic, and contented.

MOVEMENT

Development is a continuous process, which doesn't stop until the baby is full-grown. Children go through certain developmental stages. The timing may change, but the order is more or less the same for all children.

The newborn baby has a number of reflexes, such as:

• *Rooting and sucking* — When a newborn searches for the nipple after birth, he or she will turn the head to the side of the face that is being touched, grasp the nipple in his or her mouth, and start to suck.

• *Grasping* — The baby's hand will automatically clasp around an object touching the hand.

• *Startling* — At a sudden movement or noise, the baby will make a clasping motion with the arms.

• *"Walking"* — The baby will make a walking movement when the feet touch a hard surface.

The grasping, startling, and "walking" reflexes disappear after a while. They're usually gone after 3 or 4 months, when the baby begins to make more conscious motions. It's always important that a baby be able to move freely in lying-down positions (both on the tummy and on the back), so he or she can explore new movements and activities.

During the first month, the baby will usually be able to lift his or her head while lying on the tummy. Later, the baby can lift part of the chest, too, and finally the baby will pull himself or herself up by the arms. By then, he or she is probably 3 or 4 months old.

At 4 or 5 months of age, a baby can grab an object that's within reach. The eyesight has developed to the degree that he or she can "measure" distance. The baby enjoys being played with. At approximately 6 months, the baby will laugh when tickled, and just the sight of the finger coming close may be enough to trigger giggling.

The back and neck muscles gradually gain strength, and the baby will usually be able to sit up without support between 8 and 12 months.

Around 9 to 12 months of age, the baby can pull himself or herself up into a standing position while holding on to a piece of furniture, and then will "move" along the furniture.

There are great variations as to when children learn to walk, and even though some can toddle along at 9 months, most won't walk until sometime after their first birthday. The development of the feet depends somewhat on the opportunities the child has had to practice using them.

THE SENSES

The newborn's senses are more developed than previously believed. The senses help a baby explore the world, and help him or her become better coordinated. In that way, the senses and movement go hand in hand. The more you look at, touch, and hold your baby, the more he or she will explore, vocalize, and learn.

PSYCHOLOGICAL DEVELOPMENT

A child's development is closely associated with his or her understanding and intelligence, although there can be wide variations from one child to another. What's most important during the first year is that the baby feel safe and display trust.

The first smile can be seen in healthy, full-term babies sometime between the second and fifth week, or earlier.

The first words. At 9 months, the baby understands the meaning of certain words, and within the next few months starts uttering "words."

If you think that your child is late in developing, try not to rush things. Remember that development should be natural for each child. But if you are still concerned, check with your doctor.

More information about babies' psychological development is in chapter 13, on pages 82 to 89 and in the table on pages 80 to 81.

SLEEPING

The need for sleep varies greatly. From birth to 3 months, some babies sleep less than 12 hours a day, whereas others sleep a total of 20 hours! Some children sleep through the night at 2 or 3 weeks, but others need a nightly feeding for 3 or 4 months. As long as your baby seems alert and contented when awake, the number of hours doesn't much matter.

During the rest of the first year, a baby might sleep 12 hours during the night and 4 hours during the day, for a total of 16 hours. At 5 months, quiet children can still sleep for most of the day, whereas active children will want to be awake most of the time. When children are around 9 months old, they can decide for themselves whether or not they want to sleep, and they can resist the urge to fall asleep for several hours.

At 3 months, many babies have 3 or 4 periods of sleep each day. At 1 year of age, this may decline to 2 or 3 times a day. Only at 2 to 3 years of age do they tend to give up the afternoon nap.

Children sleep very deeply for the first 4 months or more. During these first months, it's difficult to disturb a child enough to wake him or her, especially right after a feeding. Later on, he or she may wake up from unusual sounds.

Sleeping positions

Recent studies suggest that the rare <u>sudden infant death syndrome</u> (or <u>crib death</u>) occurs more often with babies sleeping on the tummy than on the back or side. For this reason, always put your baby on his or her back or side when sleeping. When a baby is awake and under supervision, however, it's good for development to let him or her lie in a variety of positions.

Sleep interruptions

Children may wake up because they're thirsty (especially during the summer), because they have a wet diaper, because they are teething, because they're too cold or too hot, because their clothes are too tight, because they are overdressed, or because they have been given too much or too little food. And, they'll wake up when they're done sleeping!

Fortunately, addressing the baby's immediate need will usually solve the problem, and he or she will usually go back to sleep.

Family members needn't tip-toe around in the evening out of fear of waking the baby. Children should become accustomed to normal sounds in the home.

During the first 3 or 4 months, some children have long bouts of crying, especially in the evening and at night. If this is happening to your child, you might want to read Chapter 7, on pages 45 to 47 for a discussion about colic.

Nightmares

After about 6 months of age, your sleeping child might suddenly scream and wake up. This is probably because of some kind of a nightmare. It's generally hard to find the exact cause. However, the baby often will quiet down as soon as you attend to him or her.

THE TEETH AND TEETHING

The first <u>"milk" teeth</u> (or <u>baby teeth</u>) are already formed by the time a baby is born. So, the mother's diet and health during pregnancy are crucial for the quality of the milk teeth. On the other hand, dietary deficiencies and illness during the child's early years can greatly affect the quality of the "adult" teeth.

The timing of the appearance of teeth can vary a great deal. Once in a while (in 1 out of 2,000 cases), 1 or 2 teeth will have already emerged at birth. Some other children have their first tooth by the time they reach 3 months of age, and others at around 1 year.

Any of these timings is considered normal. The order of the appearance of teeth may vary, but is usually approximately as follows:

1. The *2 middle lower* teeth at 6 to 9 months
2. The *4 middle upper* teeth at 8 to 12 months
3. The *2 outer lower* teeth between 12 and 15 months
4. The *4 front* molars (the grinding teeth) between 14 and 16 months
5. The *4 corner* teeth (the eye teeth) at 19 to 22 months
6. The *4 back* molars at 24 to 30 months

That means that your child will have all 20 milk teeth by about 2-1/2 years of age.

During the last weeks or months before the teeth appear, babies often get itchy gums. They want to bite and rub the gums against everything, they drool constantly, and they may become irritable and whiny. Just before a tooth breaks through, you may see a blue swelling. If your child has a fever over 101 °F, something besides teething is the cause.

Can something be done to help children suffering from teething pains? It's usually much better to give them something to chew on — like hard rubber rings or frozen plastic rings filled with water — than to use medicines.

People used to believe that teething made children more prone to colds, fever, diarrhea, or cramps. Careful studies have shown that this isn't true. However, fever can sometimes speed the emergence of teeth.

TOOTH DECAY AND FLUORIDE

Tooth decay (cavities) can happen even during the early years. Teeth decay when bacteria that live in the mouth break down sugars that we eat and drink. This makes an acid that dissolves the enamel (outer coating) of the teeth and causes the decay.

Because sugars are the major cause of cavities, it's very important to keep the amount of sugars in your child's diet to a minimum. Look out for sugars in cereals, drinks, cookies, desserts, and jellies. Some fruits, such as raisins, are very high in sugars...They're nutritious for other reasons, but large quantities can harm the teeth. Another "hidden" source of sugars is some medicines. The good news is that "sugar-free" sweets, drinks, vitamins, medicines, and so forth that taste sweet *don't* cause tooth decay.

It's best not to leave your child unattended with a bottle. Give the drink, remain with the child, and then remove the bottle. Also avoid putting honey or other sweets on a pacifier. Either of these things can really damage the teeth.

It's hard to break bad habits, so try to get your child used to a healthful, sensible diet right from the start. Let him or her eat well at meal-time, and try to avoid between-meal snacking. If your child is still hungry, give a slice of bread with cheese, a vegetable, or some other food that isn't sugary or fatty. The most sensible advice is to read labels carefully, and ask your dentist or doctor for advice.

Tooth brushing should start as a game when the first teeth come through. Make sure you use the kind of small, soft brush recommended by your dentist or doctor. The toothbrushing game should become more serious when the milk molars appear, at around 18 months of age.

In addition to good tooth hygiene and a sensible low-sugar diet, fluoride is important in strengthening the teeth against tooth decay. Many water-supply systems are fluorinated (add fluoride), which helps. And, most major brands of toothpaste have fluoride. But your doctor or dentist may recommend fluoride tablets if your child is at risk for getting a lot of cavities.

THE EYES AND EYESIGHT

Infants' eyes should be the same size as each other and should look clear and shiny. The true eye color will develop toward the end of the first year.

The pupils (hole in the very middle of each eye) should be completely black and of equal size. Gray or whitish pupils may mean cataract or other eye diseases. Such problems are rare, but they do require the advice of an eye doctor as soon as possible.

If a newborn's eyes are a little crusty, it's usually quite harmless. Red eyes and larger amounts of pus may, however, be signs of a serious infection and should be examined by a doctor.

Babies don't produce many tears immediately after birth, but this will increase in the first month. At that point, some children will develop *too much* moisture in the eyes, and tears will run easily even when the child isn't crying. For some, the eyes will get pus, too, which may look sticky and dirty. This is caused by a blocked tear duct, which may open up by itself in the first year. In the meantime, your doctor may advise that you gently massage the tear sac at the inside corner of the eye.

During the first days of life, your baby's eyesight is worse than that of older children and adults, but it's still better than what people previously imagined. Even over the first few weeks, the eyesight will improve a lot, and the infant will start gazing toward visually interesting objects. Your face will probably attract the most interest.

When a baby is looking at something, the eyes should both look straight ahead and not squint. If your child doesn't start "fixing the gaze" on objects in the first month, you should talk with an eye doctor. A "shyness from light" — turning away from normal sources of light — may also indicate eye disease and should be checked by an eye doctor.

"Normal" vision is developed by around 1 year of age. In the first few years, binocular vision develops. Binocular (meaning "two-eye") vision lets us make sense of images that come from both eyes at the same time. For instance, this gives us depth perception, which means that it allows us to see in three dimensions. If you think that your baby doesn't see well, consult your doctor.

THE EARS AND HEARING

The ears are shaped to direct sound into the ear canal. At the end of the canal, there is an ear drum that vibrates when sound strikes it.

At birth, some babies' ears are covered by fine hairs. These hairs will fall out in the first month or so. If your baby has wax or other material in the ears, *never* place a cotton-tipped swab into the ear canal to try to clean it out. The swab could slip in too far or push the material deep into the canal. This can severely damage the ear drum and impair hearing.

It's been shown that babies can hear even before birth. Newborns react to loud noises by startling (see page 72). Later, they'll respond to voices by smiling or turning toward the direction of the voice. If you are concerned that your baby might have a hearing problem, see the doctor. The sooner a hearing loss is treated, the better the chance is that your child will develop normal speech and language skills.

BOWEL MOVEMENTS

During the first 3 or 4 days after birth, the infant's bowel contains a greenish-black, sticky substance called meconium. Later, the color of the stool that comes out into the diaper will depend on what the baby has had to eat or drink.

Children on breast milk have a frequent, greenish, loose, and somewhat slimy stool during the first 1 or 2 weeks. Some children have this type of bowel movement over a longer period, but most babies develop the typical mother's milk stool, which is yellow and creamy and smells pleasantly sour. Breast-fed babies sometimes have loose, greenish, slimy stools when the mother has eaten certain foods (like shellfish, cabbage, or onions). Breast-fed babies may have between 1 and 4 bowel movements each day, but there are a lot of variations. It is important to be aware that real constipation (hard stools) never occurs with breast-fed babies. Some babies go for up to 7 days between bowel movements, now and then, but the stools still will not be too hard. This "false constipation" doesn't cause the baby any discomfort, and it shouldn't be treated with enemas, suppositories, etc.

Children on formula have several "seedy" stools a day for the first several weeks. The consistency is that of scrambled eggs, and the color can vary from green to yellow. If your baby has frequent, watery stools, severe tummy aches associated with feeding, or bright red blood in the stools, contact your doctor immediately. These symptoms could be due to allergy to the formula — in which case the formula may need to be changed — or an illness requiring immediate attention.

At the transition to solid food such as cereals and soft stews, the stools get browner. They may periodically become more loose and slimy — this often happens if the baby is given too much solid food in the beginning.

Children on cow's milk (including milk-based formulas) have stools that are more solid, yellowish-white, and rotten smelling. These babies usually have 1 or 2 such bowel movements daily, but they may get constipated. Loose and frequent bowel movements are not normal, and should prompt a call to the doctor. Very white stools over a long period of time can be a sign of serious disease.

CRYING

The reasons for crying can largely be the same as those mentioned in the section called "Sleep interruptions" on page 72.

Crying can also be a "stage." Even though hunger is the most common cause for crying, a baby might also cry because of strong light in the eyes, sudden sounds, cold and heat, and so on. A baby may also cry if he or she can't move freely, kick the legs, wave the arms, or turn or lift the head. As babies grow older, they cry when they want company, and from 1-1/2 years they may show fear at being left alone in an unfamiliar place or at being approached or touched by strangers.

FINGER-SUCKING

All children will at some stage suck their fingers, especially during teething. As long as the sucking doesn't make your baby's gums sore, some doctors will tell you not to worry about it during the first year. Other doctors discourage finger-sucking because it may be a hard habit to break later on.

HEAD-BANGING AND SELF-ROCKING

A 6- to 12-month-old may start banging his or her head on the crib right after being put down to sleep. This behavior may continue until he or she is 2 or 3 years old. Treatment is usually not necessary, but head-banging may rarely be a sign of something serious. The same applies to children who sit and rock back and forth for long periods of time.

SWEATING

Some larger infants sweat from the head during sleep or feeding. This doesn't mean anything, so long as the child doesn't have a fever. You can, however, make sure that you don't over-dress your baby.

SNEEZING

Infants are nose breathers! And, in order for an infant to be able to suck — and thus to feed — he or she has to be able to breathe through the nose, too. To keep his or her nose clean, a baby will sneeze when something blocks the nose. Your baby, therefore, should sneeze. It doesn't necessarily mean that the baby has a cold.

TUMMY ACHES

Some babies get tummy aches, which may appear when the baby is 2 or 3 weeks old and last until he or she is 3 or 4 months old. The crying spells often happen between 5:00 PM and 10:00 PM. The baby may quiet down during the day and sleep well at night. When picked up during the crying spell and gently massaged on the tummy, the baby may quiet down for a while, but might then continue to cry and pull up the legs toward the chest. There is often no effective treatment for colic. Sometimes, drops that help the baby pass gas may help. (See Chapter 7 on pages 45 to 47, for more information on colic.)

PHYSICAL AND PSYCHOLOGICAL DEVELOPMENT IN THE FIRST YEAR

The following are general guidelines, with considerable variation from child to child.

AGE	DEVELOPMENT OF MOVEMENT
Newborn	Can keep the head up for a few seconds when lying on the tummy.
1 month	While on tummy or in a sitting position, can hold the head up for a very short time.
2 months	While lying on the tummy, can lift the head and part of chest well above the ground. While held in a sitting position, the head is upright but repeatedly drops forward.
3 months	When lying on the tummy and leaning on the arms, will lift both head and chest. Grabs people's hair and clothes. Can hold and move a rattle.
4 months	Can hold the head up without support. Will play for a long time with a rattle. Will grab a ring held over the chest.
5 months	Plays with toys. Held in a sitting position, will have a firm grip.
6 months	While lying on the tummy, will support self with straight arms. Can lift the head and grab the toes while lying on the back.
7 months	When lying on the back, can lift the head far up. Can also roll over from the back to the tummy. Will lift a ball on the table. Will reach for own feet. Will hold the bottle.
8 months	Will move objects from one hand to the other. Can push self backwards when lying on the tummy. Can sit up without help.
9 months	Can take a spoon and put it inside a cup. Will lean forward and regain balance. Will carry own weight when supported. May start crawling.
10 months	Will pull self up into a sitting position. Can stand with help and may walk a little while being supported.
11 months	Will pull self up into a standing position. Will walk while being supported by furniture. Can turn around and pick up an object while in a sitting position.
12 to 15 months	Will pull self into a standing position on the floor. Walks (supported by people and furniture) and gradually takes first solo steps.

PSYCHOLOGICAL DEVELOPMENT

Follows movement of parent's face for short distances. Develops eye contact during feeding.

Looks at the parents when they talk to him or her. Will watch a dangling toy. Smiles for the first time between 3 and 5 weeks.

Will follow with the eyes a person or object moving near the crib.

Smiles and giggles when being talked to. When lying on the back, will observe the hands or push a rattle.

Takes delight in the sight of toys. Displays interest when sees the bottle or the breast. Laughs out loud. Babbles in satisfied way when being pulled up into a sitting position. Will turn toward the source of a noise.

Smiles at own image in mirror. When a toy is dropped, will look for it.

Smiles and babbles with own mirror image. When a rattle is dropped, will reach out for it. Displays fear of strangers.

Pats own mirror image with hand. Tries to make contact with other people by coughing or making other sounds. Will respond to own name.

Will try for a long time to grab toys out of reach. Will react to "no."

Will imitate various sounds. Will play "pat a cake." Will wave good-bye. Starts reacting to questions like "Where is mommy?"

Will gradually understand the meaning of more words. No longer puts all objects into the mouth. Will intentionally drop objects so they can be picked up again.

Will put things into a box and take them out again. May say a "word."

Can say 2 or 3 meaningful words. Will understand the meaning of "Where is your book?" or "Where is your shoe?"

CHAPTER 13

Psychological Development

Over the past 25 years, a revolution has taken place in the understanding of infants and their psychological development. It was earlier believed that young infants couldn't comprehend or respond to their environment. Today we know that infants are interested and attentive from the very start.

THE NEWBORN ANSWERS QUESTIONS

Can 2-day-old babies recognize their own mother by her smell? To have infants "answer" this question, researchers put a breast pad moist with the mother's milk on a pillow to one side of each baby. To the other side they put a breast pad moist with milk from another woman. The infants turned their head toward their own mother's milk! When the pads were switched, the babies still turned their head toward their own mother's milk. In this way, the researchers found that infants actually recognize the smell of their own mother — and, the mother's smell was *preferred*. In this and similar ways, scientists are now better at finding what infants can do — helping infants to answer, in their own way, the questions being asked.

Video recordings have given us new opportunities to study what happens when infants and parents are together. We can watch the tapes picture by picture and study everyone's facial expressions. This has provided a new perspective on the non-verbal interplay between children and parents during the early days and weeks. Little babies participate actively in the "conversations" with their parents, conversations involving looking, smiling, and mimicking sounds and "language." Parents answer automatically in a way infants like: nice, gentle voices with rhythmic repetition and melody, and "open," expressive faces. *Contact and interplay are incredibly important for your infant's development, because it's first and foremost through interactions that babies learn about themselves and their world!*

THE NEWBORN SENSES AND REACTS

Right after birth, babies seek out impressions from their environment. Little ones can focus and follow your face when it is within about 1 foot. And, they can follow sounds with their gaze or by turning their head in the direction of the sound.

Also from birth, infants prefer certain sense impression s over others. For instance, babies prefer to look at a pattern resembling a face than other patterns. They also prefer to listen to a human voice, especially when the voice is soft and gentle.

Young infants quickly learn to distinguish between the known and the unknown. First they'll recognize their mother by her smell, then her voice, and after a few days by her face.

THE INFANT UNDERSTANDS WHOLENESS AND CONTINUITY

Newborns understand wholeness and continuity. One way they do this is to "translate" impressions from one sense to another. Amazingly, one experiment showed that 4-week-old babies could recognize by sight a certain pacifier with rubber knobs that they had earlier only felt in their mouth!

Only 3 days after birth, newborns can imitate expressions such as opening the mouth, sticking the tongue out, and moving the fingers. They can also imitate emotional impressions such as joy, fright, and surprise.

It appears that small babies comprehend and react to underlying emotional language where rhythm and movement are involved. They move rhythmically to human voices, but not to banging noises, for example. Babies are, therefore, especially responsive to songs, rocking, and movement.

VULNERABILITY

Your little child is also very vulnerable, and cannot regulate his or her own condition. The young baby often switches between sleeping and being awake, between crying and being calm. A newborn sleeps for short periods and is easily overwhelmed by stimulations when awake. This can be hunger, sleepiness, sights and sounds, or other kinds of stimulation. So, babies need to be soothed and comforted, and should be protected from overwhelming sensations. They should also be breast-fed (or bottle-fed) frequently during this period, to keep them contented and happy.

It is when babies are awake and calm that they'll express their sensory talents. In the first few weeks, this will often only happen for a few minutes. It's during these minutes that you can have eye contact and small "conversations" with the baby.

Babies who are born prematurely, or are immature in some other way, are even more sensitive to stimulations. They'll have a greater need to feel cared for and protected. It may take some weeks before the baby develops the abilities that are normally present at birth.

INFANTS ARE DIFFERENT

From the moment of birth, babies have different ways of reacting. Some find their own rhythm early on, sleep undisturbed, wake up slowly, and can withstand a lot of unrest without becoming overwhelmed.

Others are disturbed by the slightest sound, start crying, and need a long time to be soothed. These children can get into restless rhythms. If they eventually calm down at your breast, they may fall asleep before they are fully fed and will therefore wake up quickly and easily again. These infants need protection from overwhelming impressions and need some help to find a calmer rhythm.

Babies crave different things from their parents. It's important for you to understand your own baby and discover what's right for his or her own particular needs. Every infant presents challenges to his or her parents and takes part in shaping the first stages of social interplay.

TEMPERAMENT

Throughout infancy, your baby will have his or her own characteristic way of reacting. This is called temperament. We distinguish between different sides of a baby's temperament — activity level, attention span, ability to adjust, approach/withdrawal. Differences in temperament are found from early infancy. As your child grows, his or her temperament will be affected by interaction and emotional experience.

CONTACT AND INTERPLAY

Infants quickly stir up feelings in their parents and, therefore, create contact and interplay. When your little one is crying and upset, you'll want to comfort and take care of him or her. When the baby smiles, you will smile back and start a little soft chatter. This emotional language lays the foundation for future interactions.

Through emotional language, infants have their first experiences of being understood and of sharing both sorrow and joy. When your baby will not be comforted, it's easy to get frustrated or angry. It's hard to feel happy and take part in the little conversations when one is tired or fed up. Do your best to stay positive and focused on the baby, and remember that he or she is more vulnerable — and probably even more upset — than you. If you're having a lot of trouble remaining calm, or are thinking about hurting your child, *please talk to a doctor, a trusted friend, or someone at a parent support group.* Taking it out on your child will harm both of you!

ATTACHMENT AND SEPARATION

The emotional bond formed between parent and child is unique, and becomes an important "point of reference" in the child's inner world during the first year. This bond will be reflected in interactions and relationships with other people.

A newborn's ability to sense and understand allows him or her to recognize you by your smell and voice within the first week. The ability to recognize people and things develops and strengthens through interaction, and by the end of the first year a child seeks his or her parents consciously and with determination, both physically and emotionally. This search becomes especially strong when the world feels unfamiliar and overwhelming, and when the child is sick or tired. At such moments, closeness with the parents is the only thing that can comfort the child.

A sense of safety and belonging is important for children's development. At the same time, it makes them vulnerable to separation from their parents. This can show up in different ways. A 3-month-old baby's sleeping pattern might get disrupted, while a 12-month-old will cry and clearly miss his or her parents.

Longer separations can be prepared for by gradually adapting your child to them. It also eases the transition if the people who will be caring for your child know as much as possible about his or her habits and favorite toys.

DEVELOPMENT HAPPENS IN LEAPS

You will notice that the development of your baby happens in leaps and bounds, not in a steady way. This is due to changes in the brain that show themselves in psychological development and skills.

At about 2 months of age, there's usually a leap in development that, among other things, affects the baby's sleeping pattern. He or she will now usually sleep longer during the night. At the same time, the baby becomes more aware, which is expressed by longer periods of contact and interaction, and greater attentiveness.

A new leap happens at about 7 months, and again at 12 months. There's now a shift in the baby's way of interacting with other people and the way he or she explores. In particular, the abilities to cooperate and solve problems develop at these stages. A baby will, for example, learn to follow someone else's gaze, and at about 1 year will start expressing himself or herself in words.

During the first year, development happens incredibly fast...There's hardly any other period in life when one learns so much!

DEVELOPMENT AND INTERPLAY IN THE FIRST YEAR

During the first 12 months, new outlooks and experiences are created in the baby's inner world. At the same time, the baby is able to master more tasks and gets better and better at problem-solving. All these changes mean that you'll be adapting the way you interact as your child develops.

THE WORLD OF FEELINGS (MONTHS 1–2)

During the first 8 weeks, the feelings of excitement and peace are most important in the infant's world of experience. These feelings and their intensity probably impress themselves in the memory. Impressions of sight and sound, touch and movement give rise to different degrees of emotional strength.

The baby perceives shapes most easily, and will learn to use the center of the visual field. At the outer edges of the visual field, the baby can register movement. The whole experience of vision is, in a way, "variations on the same theme." Sensing the different expressions on your face is an example of this.

Bodily feelings also create inner emotions. Hunger is a very strong emotion for the young infant, and can be compared to a storm that's gathering strength! Feelings of hunger temporarily disrupt all other experiences.

COMFORT ME WHEN I CRY

When such a storm of feelings is on its way, the cry — a baby's most important way of communicating — triggers a response from the parent. You begin to talk calmly, pick the baby up, and rock or walk the baby or put him or her to the breast. This gives the youngster 4 new experiences to break the pattern: Sound, touch, movement, and a new position. The music in your voice and the rhythm in the movements help the baby to endure and calm down.

Perhaps this soft introduction is necessary for infants to feed well when they're hungry. When young babies cry and cry, they can get so excited that they need to find a peaceful rhythm in order to settle down. Once that happens, the world begins to emerge again through the senses, and the baby will recognize you and maybe fall asleep in that security.

Most parents soon learn to distinguish between different types of crying. Pain and hunger cries are especially characteristic, and parents automatically react most quickly to cries of pain. Babies will calm down fastest when only a short time has passed before comfort arrives. It's important that babies be given the chance to calm themselves down,

which sometimes they can do. However, this does *not* apply to hunger and other overwhelming needs.

A good way to soothe a newborn is to put him or her on your shoulder. This supports the baby's arms and legs, which often get restless. Together with the upright position, this also makes the child open his or eyes. A steady, rhythmic movement — paired with your voice — can help your baby find a calmer state of being.

The near social world (months 2–5)

At around 2 months of age, the infant's talent for social contact will really bloom. Smiles can now be controlled, and the child starts using smiles as greetings. He or she also starts to babble, and can keep eye contact over a longer period of time.

Your little one is finding great pleasure and interest in face-to-face contact, and it seems that he or she is learning to understand what different facial expressions mean. Never will social contact be more important than now! An 8-week-old baby is attracted to shapes and movement on the face itself, whereas during the newborn period he or she followed the edges of the face.

However, your facial expressions are not the only reason that faces are so important. The face also reflects what the *baby* is doing from one moment to the next. This feedback helps the baby understand that there's a connection between the self and the face.

During this period, a joy in learning about his or her own actions and the ability to affect the environment also develop. These are shown in many ways. Babies may, for example, quickly learn that they can move a hanging mobile with their foot, and take great delight in the resulting motions.

In each other's gaze

Nothing can compare to the delight of eye contact! It seems as if these small "conversations" are mainly about observing each other and exchanging feelings and looks. It's like the infant sees the eyes as "the mirror of the soul." So, eye contact is an important way for the baby to establish a sense of belonging.

Happy smiles and babble belong to this period, too. Then the baby — by looks, expressions, and movements — conveys "That's enough; I need a little break." Small breaks are an important way infants control the impressions they receive.

When a mother talks to her baby, she conveys clear messages with her looks and expressions: "So, you like talking to your mommy. What are you going to tell me today, then?" As the child grows older, small games like "peek-a-boo" and variations of "I'm coming to get you" become part of the interplay that the child happily participates in.

A WHOLE WORLD OF PEOPLE AND THINGS (MONTHS 5–12)

From around 5 months, infants become more and more aware of the world around them, and are more engaged in *exploring.* Motor skills and coordination are continuing to develop, and babies learn to grab, shake, bang, and let go. They explore objects they've gotten hold of: Can it move? Does it make a sound? In the second half of the first year, children start to move around, which gives all sorts of new opportunities for exploration.

At this time, infants can clearly distinguish between people they know and strangers. At first this happens through increased interest and the need to explore. Then, at 6 to 7 months, a change takes place. The contact is more hesitant and expectant, and your child may reject and withdraw from strangers. This fear of strangers shows that the child is aware of an attachment to the people he or she normally associates with.

Children this age will also be cautious toward everything unknown, be it sounds, objects, places, or people. The more overwhelming the unknown, the more frightening the experience. *At such times, parents' arms are the best place from which to explore!*

LET'S DISCOVER THE WORLD TOGETHER

Gradually an interest for discovering the world *with* another person develops. This happens at around 7 months of age, when the child is developing an ability to follow someone else's gaze. At about 9 months, the baby learns to point, and he or she understands that a pointed finger indicates the direction to something.

Eye contact is no longer quite as important to your baby. Instead it's the fact that *both* of you have your attention directed toward the same object. Pointing becomes a way of inviting you to join in a journey of discovery. Parents and other close people become companions while the child is discovering the world. A new game, a new way of togetherness develops.

Eye contact and facial expressions are still important, but now they're only part of the way of making contact. Looks reassure your child that "Now we're looking at this together" or "We're interested in the same thing." Facial expressions tell the child what you're feeling. It's as if he or she starts understanding that people have inner feelings.

In fact, children this age use adult facial expressions as a way of interpreting the world. The expressions show what's safe and what may be dangerous, and also what's fun! The joy of these little games have now surpassed the delights of eye contact.

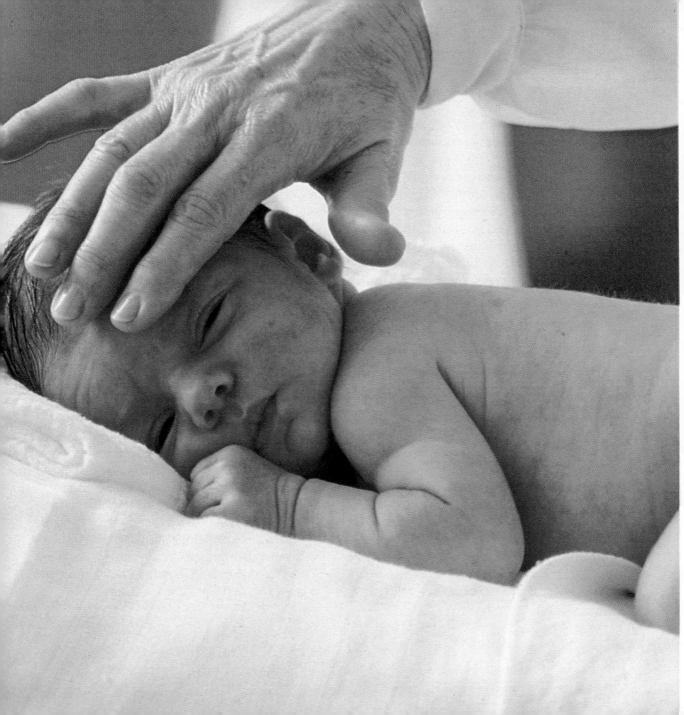

CHAPTER 14

Baby's Checkups and Immunizations

HEALTH CHECKUPS

Luckily, very few children are born with major birth defects or illnesses. Most babies are born in hospitals or birthing centers, where a thorough medical examination will take place shortly after the birth. Therefore, a lot of problems can be detected early. But many new mothers still worry that something might be wrong with their baby, or feel insecure about caring for their child. If so, it's better to ask the doctor or nurse about something than to worry unnecessarily!

All infants and children should be checked regularly by a doctor or nurse, throughout childhood. Your doctor's office or health clinic will have officially recommended checkup schedules on hand. Because every child is unique, the official guidelines may be adjusted somewhat for your own child. In general, the checkups (also called well-baby visits) happen frequently — perhaps every few weeks — for the first 6 months. During the second half of the first year, they are usually scheduled somewhat less frequently.

At the checkups, your baby will be weighed and measured. Other tests will be taken, too, and you'll be offered advice about baby care, breast-feeding, nutrition, and safety. The necessary vaccinations will also be given.

You'll probably have questions, but it's easy to forget what you wanted to ask once you're actually at the doctor's office or clinic. So, it's a good idea to write down any questions or concerns beforehand.

Be reassured that everything will probably be fine at the well-baby visits. However, it's important to keep to the recommended schedule, so that anything out of the ordinary can be found as soon as possible. As the saying goes, prevention is the best remedy!

Vaccinations

Vaccines are given to help prevent certain contagious diseases, or at least to decrease the severity of the diseases if the person catches them. Vaccines contain infectious agents (such as viruses or bacteria) that have been specially treated to make the vaccines as safe as possible. The process of giving vaccines is called vaccination or immunization.

Some diseases that used to kill or harm hundreds or thousands of children each year — diseases such as smallpox — have been completely eliminated or dramatically reduced, thanks to widespread vaccination efforts. It's important that your child be immunized, on time, as recommended by your doctor or clinic. Your health care professional will explain to you, in detail, the symptoms of the diseases and the benefits and risks of vaccination.

Almost all infants should be vaccinated against the following diseases: diphtheria, tetanus, and pertussis; measles, mumps, and rubella; polio; and Haemophilus b. Some babies should also be vaccinated against chickenpox, hepatitis B, and/or hepatitis A.

It would seem desirable to vaccinate children shortly after birth. However, this isn't recommended, because a child's ability to form protective antibodies from the vaccines is low if he or she is vaccinated before 2 months of age. You should also know that many vaccines need to be given several times to be truly effective.

DTP vaccine

The DTP vaccine is a combination vaccine that helps protect against three diseases: diphtheria, tetanus (lockjaw), and pertussis (whooping cough).

This vaccine is injected into a muscle. Your child may be slightly irritable for a few hours after the injection, and may develop a slight fever, which usually disappears the next day. The area around the injection site might be a little sore and red. Sometimes, a small lump under the skin can be felt, but it should go away shortly. If your baby develops a high fever or cries inconsolably after the injection, call the doctor or clinic.

Diphtheria is rare nowadays in industrialized countries such as ours. If, however, the vaccine were to be discontinued, diphtheria would probably infect large numbers of people after a few years. That is why children should continue to be vaccinated against diphtheria. Symptoms of diphtheria include high fever, very sore throat, and difficulty breathing. It requires immediate medical attention.

Tetanus (or lockjaw) has gradually become more rare, too, but the cases that do occur can be very serious. When people get the disease, their face muscles become paralyzed and they can't open their mouth or swallow. The paralysis then spreads. Tetanus is found in some rusty metals and in some soils, especially soil contaminated with animal droppings. If a child has an open wound such as a cut, the tetanus can get into his or her body. A "booster dose" will probably be given if a person is exposed to tetanus but hasn't had a tetanus shot in the past 6 or 7 years.

Pertussis (or whooping cough) remains a serious disease for infants, and can occur as an epidemic, i.e., infecting many children at a time. When this disease occurs, the person gets "fits" of coughing that last for minutes on end, has trouble breathing, and may even vomit or burst some blood vessels from the intensity of the coughing. If an infant is exposed to whooping cough before he or she can be vaccinated, the vaccine will probably no longer be effective. The baby will be given a special gamma globulin treatment instead of the vaccine. The child will then be protected against whooping cough for about 1 month.

MMR VACCINE

The MMR vaccine is a combination vaccine against measles, mumps, and rubella (German measles). Some children will develop a slight fever, mild rash, soreness in the joints, and/or swollen lymph glands under the jaw in the first couple of weeks after the injection. These symptoms should go away quickly. If you notice stronger reactions, contact the doctor or clinic immediately.

Measles is rarely seen now, because most children get vaccinated against it. Symptoms include very high fever, severe cough, runny nose, red eyes, and a tell-tale red rash that often starts behind the ears and spreads to the rest of the body.

Mumps affects glands under the jaw, just below the ears. When someone gets mumps, these glands swell up and get quite painful. The person might also have a fever. Although the infection itself may seem mild, mumps can cause long-term problems in some people, especially adolescents or adults. Therefore, it's important to immunize against mumps as soon and as often as your doctor or clinic recommends.

Rubella (or German measles) is a disease that causes a low fever, runny nose, mild cough, swollen glands at the back of the head, and a light pink rash that often starts at the hairline and then spreads over the body. Although it tends to be a mild illness in children, rubella frequently produces severe birth defects if a pregnant woman catches the disease. By immunizing all children, years before they grow up and have children of their own, doctors hope to eliminate this situation.

POLIO VACCINE

Your baby will probably receive several doses of a vaccine against polio. The vaccine might be injected, or it might be given orally (by mouth). Polio used to be widespread, but vaccination has practically eliminated it in this country. With polio, various parts of the nervous system are affected, and the person may become permanently paralyzed.

HiB VACCINE

The HiB vaccine helps protect children (and adults) against one type of bacteria. The bacteria, called *Haemophilus influenzae* type b, causes meningitis (inflammation of the covering of the brain and spinal cord), pneumonia, and other very serious infections. The vaccine rarely has "side effects," except for temporary redness or soreness at the injection site.

CHICKENPOX VACCINE

There is now a vaccine against chickenpox, too. Chickenpox may be very uncomfortable, producing a low fever, cough, and characteristic bumps on the skin that are very itchy. The bumps — called pox — can lead to skin infections and scarring if scratched. The pox can spread all over the body. Most children who get chickenpox recover completely, but the disease can be more serious in adolescents and adults.

HEPATITIS B VACCINE

Hepatitis B is an infection of the liver. It is transmitted through the blood or other body fluids. People with hepatitis B may feel fine, or they may feel very ill, with loss of appetite, weight loss, vomiting, and jaundice (yellowing of the skin and eyes). Whether or not the person gets symptoms, hepatitis B can be very serious, and it may linger throughout the person's life. Vaccination may be recommended for infants (and others) who are at high risk for getting hepatitis B.

HEPATITIS A VACCINE

Hepatitis A is another type of liver infection. It may not make the person sick for as long as hepatitis B, but can be very contagious. Hepatitis A may be transmitted in many different ways, including through raw or under-cooked foods. Vaccination against hepatitis A may or may not be recommended for your child.

Baby's Immunization Schedule

AGE	VACCINES	DATE
2 months	DTP, Polio, HiB	_____
4 months	DTP, Polio, HiB	_____
6 months	DTP, Polio, HiB	_____
12–15 months	DTP, Polio, HiB, MMR, tuberculosis	_____
4–6 years	DTP, Polio	_____
11–12 years	MMR	_____
14–16 years	Diphtheria and tetanus	_____
Every 10 years	Diphtheria and tetanus	_____
	Hepatitis A vaccine	_____
	Hepatitis B vaccine	_____
	Chickenpox vaccine	_____
		_____
		_____

CHAPTER 15

When Baby's Sick

THE HEALTHY NEWBORN

At birth, your baby leaves the protective world of your womb, where warmth, oxygen, and nourishment were always available. The newborn is suddenly exposed to all sorts of new and changing conditions. There will be different temperatures; various sights, smells, and sounds; exposure to infections; and a range of new processes within his or her little body.

Dramatic changes will be happening in the respiratory system, circulatory system, and digestive system. So, it's natural that some time will pass before everything is fully functional and in balance. Your baby will make a lot of adjustments to the "outside world" over the first few months, and development will continue throughout life! But these developments occur naturally and without problems in most babies, and you don't need to be a professional to be a good mother.

The lungs

One of the most dramatic changes a newborn experiences is breathing air. Most babies take their first breath within 30 seconds of being born. Others may take a bit longer, because during birth they received little oxygen or their mother took certain medications.

Young infants often have an uneven breathing pattern. Fortunately, newborns can cope better with short periods of oxygen deficiency than older children and adults can.

The heart

When the umbilical cord is cut, the blood flow from you to your child ends. When your baby takes that first breath, the blood flow in his or her heart and blood vessels changes, and circulation of blood to the lungs begins.

The liver

The liver has several functions. One of its functions is to break down and secrete bilirubin, the yellow coloring made when red blood cells break down as a normal part of living. Before this process starts, bilirubin accumulates in the body, so many newborns develop jaundice (yellow skin) during the first week of life. The jaundice may go away on its own. Feeding the baby 8 or more times in 24 hours also reduces it. Alternatively, some children are treated on a "light bed," where they lie under special ultraviolet light bulbs or in sunlight.

The kidneys

A baby's kidneys start producing urine toward the end of the first trimester of pregnancy. Before birth, your baby's waste products were discarded mainly through you or became part of the amniotic fluid. At birth, the kidneys become fully active, and the first urine is usually excreted shortly after birth. There might not be much urine during the first few days, but it increases as your child starts feeding.

The umbilical cord

The umbilical cord stump usually dries up and falls off in the first 1 or 2 weeks after birth. Once the stump falls off, it takes a few days before the navel (belly button) area is covered by new skin. Infections can get into the new navel. If it oozes, it should be cleaned carefully— your doctor will tell you how.

The belly button usually heals without any problems, although a "plug" sometimes forms. This looks like dead skin and may leak a tiny amount of bloody liquid. Don't worry, this is not usually dangerous and it is easily treated.

Weight loss

Most newborns lose 5% to 10% of their birth weight in the first 3 days. Their weight usually starts to go up after that, when your breast milk production is fully established. If your baby feeds well, his or her birth weight may be regained in 7 to 10 days. This could take longer, however, and the weight gain may not follow a steady pattern. Talk to your doctor if your child doesn't seem to be gaining enough weight.

Body temperature

The body temperature of newborn children is about 98.6°F. For some babies, the temperature increases to 99.5°F to 101.5°F as the body weight starts to climb. This rise in temperature may be due to lack of fluids, not infection.

It's important to know that infants can't control their body temperature. Young children may display a fever without being ill, and they may be ill without getting a fever. *Measuring the temperature is an unreliable measure of illness during infancy....Behavior is a better indicator.* That said, a persistent or very high fever should be checked by the doctor.

Babies tend to lose a great deal of heat. Being underdressed can make their temperature sink too low, and they can't increase their body temperature by shivering. (Crying is one way infants can generate heat.) Conversely, an "artificial fever" can be produced by wrapping the baby in too many clothes and covers.

Hormones

During pregnancy, both boys and girls are affected by their mother's hormones. It may take a little time for newborns' hormones to adjust. During the first few weeks, some gray-white mucus may come out of the vagina of baby girls. After 5 or 6 days, some bloody mucus might also be there.

Both boys and girls may, towards the end of the first week of life, get swollen breast glands. Some liquid resembling breast milk may even leak out. This breast swelling usually goes away after a few weeks.

Birth swelling and head molding

Many children develop swelling on the part of the body that first emerged at birth. Because most babies are born head first, this birth swelling is most commonly on the head. This *does not* usually mean that the area is damaged. The swelling normally disappears on its own.

Because the baby's head needs to fit through the birth canal, it may be somewhat misshapen at birth. This usually goes away soon.

Problems at birth

Most babies are born healthy and complete. Unfortunately, some newborns do have medical problems. A doctor can detect many of those problems immediately after birth.

Some birth defects and illnesses are inherited, whereas others may have happened during the pregnancy or birth. In many cases, it isn't possible to find a definitive cause. Birth defects can occur anywhere in the body — including the heart, bones, nervous system, or urinary tract. Genetic problems can be inherited from one or both parents, even if both parents are healthy.

The basic organ systems are formed during the first 3 months of pregnancy. They are especially vulnerable during that time. Poor nutrition, medicines, infections, alcohol, smoking, and x-rays are just some of the things that may cause permanent deformities.

Previously, lack of oxygen during birth was believed to be the cause of brain damage or cerebral palsy. It is now known that most brain damage actually occurrs in premature infants after birth, and in full-term infants before labor or admission to the hospital. Even if some damage has happened, the child might grow up to be healthy and normal.

FEVERS AND INFECTIONS

Small children can very easily develop a high temperature without being particularly ill. The most common cause of fever is infection, usually of the throat or nose. Increasing the temperature is one way the body tries to resist infectious bacteria and viruses.

A baby's temperature typically ranges between 97.5 °F and 99.5 °F. Some children have even greater changes in their normal body temperature. Temperatures are lowest at night and highest in the afternoon. Putting your hand on a child's forehead is not a reliable way to measure temperature. Your baby will have to get used to having his or her temperature taken with a thermometer inserted into the rectum (bottom) or in the armpit.

Of even greater importance than measuring the temperature is *observing your baby*. Signs that he or she may not be well include the following: appearing "limp" and sluggish; not wanting to sit up, to talk, to play, or to eat or drink; and not getting any better after receiving fever-reducing medicines.

Children with fever have poor appetite. Don't force your child to eat, but do make sure that he or she drinks plenty of fluids (liquids).

When children are vomiting or have diarrhea, the fluid intake must be increased even more to replace the fluids they are losing. Weak tea, mineral water, or water with sugar are recommended. Avoid milk and juices.

If your child is nauseous, give fluids in small amounts. It may be easier for him or her to take sips through a straw than straight out of a glass. Older children can suck on ice chips, too. Popsicles™ frozen snacks and carbonated beverages (such as soda) contain useful amounts of fluids and may be more appetizing to a sick child than many other foods. It's more important for your child to drink than to eat. When he or she is no longer nauseous, you can give crackers, pretzels, mashed potatoes, or dry white toast, then gradually progress to the normal diet.

If your baby or child refuses to stay in bed with a fever, it's probably fine to let him or her get up for a while. However, he or she shouldn't be allowed outdoors and shouldn't be exposed to hot or cold rooms. Dress the baby warmly enough, but not too warmly.

It is *not* always necessary to use fever-reducing medicines. In many cases, babies can maintain a surprisingly good state of well-being even with a temperature of 104 °F! However, you should contact your doctor to make sure. To bring down fevers, you may be told to put your child into a tub of room-temperature water. It's also important to keep an eye out for symptoms of serious infections. For

example, infections such as <u>meningitis</u> (an inflammation of the brain covering) can seem like regular viral infections at first.

Often, appetite and fluid intake improve with fever-reducing medicines such as <u>acetaminophen</u>. (<u>Aspirin</u> is *not* recommended.) Store medicines safely and follow the recommended dosages exactly. Giving too much medicine — or the right amount too frequently — can cause serious poisoning!

Febrile seizures

Approximately 1 out of 20 infants and toddlers will have at least one <u>febrile (fever) seizure</u> from high body temperature. Febrile seizures usually affect children between the ages of 6 months and 5 years. During that period, the brain is especially sensitive to high temperature, particularly if the temperature is rising rapidly. The child stiffens and may faint, the eyes roll, the jaws clench tightly together, and the body jerks. Such an attack may last from a few seconds to 10 or 15 minutes.

Treatment of febrile seizures usually consists of cooling the child down. Undress your child and place a towel with cool (but not freezing) water on the forehead or around the body, especially in the armpits, around the neck, and on the groin. Don't put your finger or other object into his or her mouth. Do turn the child onto one side so that he or she doesn't choke on or breathe in any vomit. Call the doctor, who will give other emergency advice and will try to determine the cause of the fever. He or she will probably tell you to give the child a fever-reducing medicine such as acetaminophen. If your child has had febrile seizures before, the doctor may have prescribed medicine to be inserted into the rectum. This treatment usually works within a short time.

Infections

Most infections are caused by viruses or by bacteria. Children can become infected even before or during birth. Premature babies and those who had complicated births are particularly vulnerable.

Toward the end of pregnancy, you pass a range of antibodies to your baby. The antibodies provide *temporary* protection against certain infections, especially against "childhood diseases" such as measles, mumps, rubella, and chickenpox. However, the natural protection only lasts about 2 months — after that, *vaccination is essential* (see Chapter 14, "Baby's Checkups and Immunizations," pages 91 to 95.) Children who are breast-fed receive specific antibodies through mother's milk, which also provides protection against digestive system infections.

Because of the antibodies, breast-fed newborns seldom get infectious illnesses other than colds and some infections of the digestive system. Most nose and throat infections during this period are caused by viruses, which means that antibiotics are rarely needed.

It's hard to prevent all infections in infants and toddlers. Babies who have older sisters and brothers, in particular, are constantly exposed to infectious substances. It may be comforting to know that babies do gradually build up their own defense system against infections.

EAR, NOSE, THROAT, AND RESPIRATORY PROBLEMS

It's common for children to get respiratory infections, with a runny nose and a sore throat. Older children may develop a cough, whereas infants do not generally cough much when suffering from a cold. Colds are usually caused by viruses, which are spread by droplets from others (such as by coughing and sneezing). Viruses usually take 1 to 3 days before symptoms are seen. Nose and throat infections usually run their course in less than a week.

Feeling cold or being in cold weather *doesn't* cause colds; however, it may reduce a person's resistance to infection. Children needn't stay in bed when they have a normal cold. Give plenty of fluids, and give nose drops, if necessary, to ease breathing.

If the tonsils become infected and swollen, eating may become a problem, and your child may develop a sore, painful throat. When the adenoids of the throat are infected and swollen, the child's nose may also become blocked, and he or she may snore and breathe with an open mouth. Enlarged adenoids may lead to ear infections.

Croup

Croup is inflammation of the larynx (voice box) of the throat that causes a hoarse, barking cough. It usually appears in connection with a normal cold. Symptoms often show up immediately after the child has gone to bed in the evening. The coughing leads to difficulty breathing, and inhalation (breathing in) becomes strained and hoarse, often with an unusual, jarring noise. Some babies get croup several times during their childhood, but the condition becomes rarer as the child grows older.

Treatment consists of calming the child, raising the main part of the body, and having the child breathe moist air. The easiest way to do this is to take your child into the bathroom and let him or her breathe the steam from a hot shower. (Don't put the child into the hot water!) Drinking plenty of cool juice or water may also help reduce symptoms. Medicines are not generally advised at first, but do call the doctor or go to the hospital if the breathing difficulties become severe or if they don't improve quickly.

Ear infection

Ear infections are very common in youngsters. Often the symptoms are associated with a cold, but they may also be the only sign of an infection. Children typically hold their ear or turn their head from side to side.

The pain in the ears may become intense, and it may last for several days. Your child might be soothed by lying with his or her head high up. Acetaminophen can be used for both relieving pain and reducing fever. Ear infections are usually treated with antibiotics. If the eardrum ruptures, pus may leak out from the ear. This should be looked at by a doctor as soon as possible. Letting pus or fluid stay in the middle ear might cause hearing problems.

Bronchitis

An infection can sometimes spread from the upper respiratory system — such as the nose and throat — down to the airway tubes, which are called the bronchi. During the first year of life, one kind of viral infection of the bronchi causes asthma-like symptoms, with strained, panting breathing. Some babies get so short of breath that they have to be admitted to the hospital. Older children may develop a troublesome cough. Treatment often consists of keeping the child indoors and letting him or her rest for a few days. A cough syrup that breaks up mucus may also help.

Pneumonia

Pneumonia is an inflammation of the lungs. It can be caused by viruses or by bacteria. Symptoms include high temperature, rapid breathing, deep cough, and maybe pain in the chest. These symptoms can be worse if the pneumonia is accompanied by a cold. If you suspect pneumonia, you should call the doctor immediately.

GASTROINTESTINAL SYMPTOMS

Digestive system problems are very common in infants and toddlers. Problems may range from vomiting, to tummy pains, to changes in the stools, to appendicitis.

Vomiting

Regurgitation (spitting up) frequently happens in infancy, and often means that the baby has eaten too quickly or too much. Vomiting may also have causes entirely outside the stomach and intestines. For example, urinary tract infection in infants and toddlers may show up as nausea and vomiting.

Violent vomiting — possibly to the extent that the vomit is projected across the room — might indicate a narrowing in the passage between the stomach and the small intestine. This projectile vomiting is more common in boys than in girls. Symptoms usually occur a few weeks after birth. If the episodes are indeed caused by a narrowing, the child will need surgery.

For some children, spitting up and vomiting may go on past the first 6 months, and they become habitual regurgitators. Some babies seem to enjoy the regurgitation and almost "feed" on it. They may stick their fingers in their mouth or use their tongue to bring it on. If this continues, it can cause weight loss and other health problems. In that case, you should talk to the doctor.

Stomach pain

The cause of pain in the stomach or abdomen of a child may be very difficult to determine. It could be caused by colic, in which case a gentle massage and gas-relieving medication often help. Turn to Chapter 7, pages 45 to 47, and Chapter 8, pages 49 to 51 for more information about colic and baby massage.

If the pain is around the belly button and isn't associated with fever, diarrhea, vomiting, or other symptoms, it probably shouldn't concern you unless it continues. However, if the pain is in another part of the abdomen or your child has other symptoms, you should definitely contact your doctor.

Babies who are given breast milk sometimes react to foods their mother eats. Foods that give adults indigestion can also give breast-fed infants a tummy ache. These foods include onions, cabbage, grapes, and citrus fruits, as well as chocolates, nuts, and other fruits, and the caffeine in coffee, tea, and some other beverages.

If you are bottle-feeding your baby, check that the hole in the nipple is the right size, so that the formula doesn't flow out too quickly or too slowly. Babies who suck in too much air when feeding may get stomach pains.

Change in bowel movements

A breast-feeding child may have made a bowel movement every time you change the diaper, or as rarely as once a week. Either of these is normal. If your child seems contented, has no stomach pains, and gains weight well, the frequency of bowel movements is not important.

However, infants can become constipated from drinking too much cow's milk (including cow's milk formulas). Constipation often occurs with stomach pain and discomfort during bowel movement. The first option to consider is a change of diet. Laxatives should *not* be used unless you've consulted the doctor first.

Diarrhea is frequent, loose, watery stools. Some children have frequent bowel movements without diarrhea. The most common cause of diarrhea is stomach infection, often with a fever and vomiting. Such stomach infections should be taken seriously, because a child can become dehydrated within a short time. Signs of dehydration include having a dry diaper for more than 8 to 10 hours, a dry tongue, and sunken eyes. A child with stomach infection should avoid cow's milk, most juices, and foods with fiber in them. Breast-feeding can be continued. Treatment consists of sugar water, commercial preparations specific for babies' diarrhea, or carbonated drinks. Write down how much the child is drinking, and try to keep track of approximately how much of it your child is expelling. If vomiting and diarrhea persist, and your child shows signs of dehydration, you should call the doctor.

Some children may continue to produce loose stools — stools that are very plentiful, are strong smelling, and have a fatty-looking shine. This may indicate that nutrients aren't being absorbed well enough in the intestines. Typically, children with such stools have a noticeably protruding stomach and thin arms and legs. They should be examined by a doctor for malnutrition.

Bloody stools can be a sign of intestinal infection or a tear in the rectum. It's possible for a doctor to locate such tears. If your child has a large amount of fresh blood in the stools, the doctor should be called *immediately*. If the child also has stomach pains and cries inconsolably, he or she might have a severe twisting of the intestines. This condition is serious if it lasts for more than a few hours.

Pinworms are common in small children and toddlers. A child with pinworms may wake up during the night with an itchy bottom. Small worms emerge at night from the rectum and appear in large numbers around the rectal opening. The worms are white, about 1/2 inch long, and as thin as thread. The worms and their eggs can be found everywhere and are spread by flies. The eggs get into the child's body through the mouth, and hatch in the intestines. Treatment to eliminate pinworms is simple — medicines are available at pharmacies. All family members should be treated.

Hernia

Hernia is a condition in which part of one of the organs in the abdomen swells out through a weak point in the abdominal wall. The most common type is umbilical hernia, which may become hard and tight when the child is crying. The child doesn't suffer and doesn't need to receive treatment. This hernia usually heals itself within the first year of life.

Inguinal hernia is more common in boys than girls, and more common with premature than full-term babies. It appears as a bulge in the groin area or in the testicles. Such hernias get larger and harder when the child cries. If the child keeps crying and suffers pain, and the hernia does not go back into place, immediate surgery is required.

An uncomplicated hernia that doesn't show signs of being "stuck" can be treated with a simple operation and a brief hospital stay.

CHANGES OF THE SKIN

Many newborns have small, yellow-white spots on the skin, usually on the nose and forehead. This is not a sign of infection. It will disappear without treatment.

Birth marks may be found anywhere on the body, but in newborns they are most often over the nose and on the back of the head. These will probably go away on their own. Another type of birth mark is hemangiomas. They are violet in color and may seem frightening, but will usually disappear within a couple of years. It is *very rare* to come across malignant (dangerous) birth marks in children.

During the first months of life, a mild eczema or "cradle cap" is common. Children develop a thick fatty layer on their scalp and other places. This usually disappears with gentle scrubbing with a soapy cloth or with a mild cortisone cream from the pharmacy. Atopic eczema normally appears later in the first year. It is characterized by a red, itchy rash on the cheeks, and especially on the back of the arms and legs. Atopic eczema can flare up due to food and other allergies. If your child has eczema, and allergy runs in the family, you may be advised to avoid milk, eggs, and dairy prod-ucts. Children with eczema should use a special neutral soap.

Diaper rash is a skin irritation caused by the ammonia in urine. The skin is red and irritated, and frequently swollen and rough. The risk of diaper rash is greatest if the child lies for a long time in a wet diaper. You can use a protective cream at each diaper change to help prevent diaper rash, too. Sometimes a child may get a fungal infection in which the skin becomes bright red and looks irritated, with white peeling flakes. This should be looked at by a doctor.

Impetigo (milk blotch) is a contagious skin infection caused by bacteria. Impetigo can start in small cuts or sores, often around the mouth. It may look like eczema or chicken-pox if scratched severely. Impetigo is treated with an antibacterial cream or antibiotics.

Hives are an immediate sensitivity reaction of the skin. They're rare in infants, but relatively common in older children. Hives are a rash of uneven white spots surrounded by red skin. The rash can appear anywhere on the body, and is very itchy. The throat may also swell up, causing the child difficulty in breathing. Breathing or swallowing problems require *immediate* medical attention! Hives are sometimes brought on by medicines, but usually the cause remains unknown. The itchiness can be somewhat soothed by allergy medicine or natural homeopathic medicine, if your doctor recommends it.

Heat rash appears when a baby is too hot. It looks like small red spots, which disappear when the baby cools down.

Thrush is a whitish coating on the tongue and in the mouth. It is common in infants and is due to a fungal infection. Thrush often appears after antibiotic treatment. Thrush in the mouth is harmless and does disappear with antifungal medicines.

TEETHING

Teething can be uncomfortable, and may cause your child to be restless and irritable. However, there is no foundation for believing that teething causes raised temperature in children. If teething is associated with or followed by fever, it usually means that an infection has occurred, and a doctor should be consulted.

URINARY TRACT TROUBLES

Urinary tract infections are relatively uncommon in infants, but they can occur. Because babies can't complain of pain as they urinate, it may be hard to determine whether the symptoms stem from the urinary tract. It's also difficult to notice whether an infant is urinating more frequently than usual. Vomiting, loss of appetite and weight, and general lack of well-being may be symptoms of urinary tract infection. The urine should always be examined by a doctor when a possible infection is accompanied by fever.

Tight foreskin can, for some boys, cause a swelling like a "balloon" at the tip of the penis during urination. If the foreskin is so tight that it causes problems during urination or infections of the foreskin, surgery may be required. Otherwise, the foreskin may be turned back and washed, but don't pull the skin so far back that it tears. Circumcision — the surgical removal of the foreskin — may be performed as part of a religious or social ritual — but there's no medical reason for doing it routinely.

COMMON CHILDHOOD DISEASES

Several of the following "childhood diseases" are becoming more rare as children receive immunization by vaccination. (See Chapter 14, "Baby's Checkups and Immunizations," pages 91 to 95, for more information about vaccinations.)

Measles starts out as a "cold" with a runny nose, dry cough, and fever. The child's eyes become red and irritated, and a rash appears after 2 to 3 days. The incubation period — the time between infection and the beginning of symptoms — is about 7 to 10 days. If a child is exposed to infection before he or she has been vaccinated, gamma globulin can be given within 72 hours, which may prevent the development of the disease.

Mumps is characterized by fever and swelling of the salivary (spit) glands in front of the ears. Mumps is caused by a virus with an incubation period of 17 to 21 days. The illness can be almost symptom-free, or it can produce considerable swelling plus pain and fever.

Rubella (German measles) symptoms include a runny nose, slight fever, and achy joints. After 2 or 3 days, a pale red rash of small spots covers the entire body. The child develops swollen and sore lymph glands, especially in the back of the neck. The incubation period is 1 to 3 weeks.

Chickenpox often starts with a fever (100.5°F to 102.5°F) and a rash of small individual red spots that blister within hours. The rash is very itchy, so it may be soothing to rub some calamine lotion on the rash. Remember to trim your child's nails short to prevent him or her from cutting open the skin with scratching. Incubation takes 2 to 3 weeks.

Whooping cough begins as a cold, with runny nose and cough. There is no fever, or only a very slight temperature. Within 3 weeks, the cough is accompanied by "whooping" and vomiting, especially during the night. The cough then goes away within a couple more weeks. The illness is caused by bacteria, and the incubation period is 1 to 2 weeks. Unfortunately, it's usually hard for the doctor to diagnose whooping cough early enough for antibiotics to be effective.

Scarlet fever normally starts with fever, sore throat, and swollen, red tonsils. After about 24 hours, red spots appear, often first on the inside of the thighs. Typical characteristics are red cheeks, a red "raspberry" tongue, and a pale triangle around the mouth. Scarlet fever may cause inflamed kidneys. The incubation period is 2 to 3 days. Scarlet fever is caused by bacteria called streptococci that respond very well to penicillin.

Three-day-fever (roseola) is an illness mainly affecting children 6 months to 3 years of age. It causes high fever for about 3 days, commonly with a red throat, too. After 3 days, the temperature suddenly drops, coinciding with a light spotty rash covering the whole body. The disease is caused by a virus, and is not particularly contagious. Neither does it require any special treatment.

CHAPTER 16

In Safe Hands

From the time your child is 4 months old until he or she is about 2 years old, an enormous amount of development happens. Your baby is no longer a little bundle, but is learning to sit, crawl, and walk. He or she moves around, tastes, and explores — making new discoveries and accomplishing new tasks each day! It's an exciting — and exhausting — time for both of you!

When children are moving from one developmental stage to another, the risk of accidents is greatest. Little ones are full of enthusiasm and energy. At the same time, they don't have full control over their movements yet, and they're just learning how to judge what's safe and what's dangerous.

PREVENTION IS KEY!

The best way to deal with injuries is to try to prevent them from happening. Of course, accidents can't always be prevented. You should prepare as best you can, and try to make your home safe and secure. On the other hand, it's not healthy to overprotect your child from learning experiences. Letting a child explore — within limits — is good for him or her, and makes your day easier, too.

It's important to *think prevention* in any situation. Look around your home from a "baby's eye view." What hazards are within reach? Are there sharp corners on tables? Open electrical outlets? Chemicals and medicines in unlocked cabinets? There are a lot of things that may not be obvious at first... You may wish to consider taking a course in safety, first aid, and cardiopulmonary resuscitation (CPR) at your local Red Cross, police or fire department, school, or "the Y." Excellent books also exist. Your doctor may be able to recommend some sources, or try the Yellow Pages and bookstores.

Also, remember to keep the phone numbers for the doctor, hospital, police, fire, and poison control center by each telephone.

FALLS

Infants and children will have their share of falls by the time they're grown. Even the most careful parent — and most cautious child — can't prevent all accidents. However, you can try to stop them. In particular, serious injuries can happen from falls down stairs, out windows, and off furniture.

Head injuries are common, but luckily, few are serious. Preventing damage to the brain is the most important consideration. When a baby falls down, there is usually a moment's silence before the crying starts. If the child stays conscious, calms down after a few minutes, has normal skin color, and does not vomit, it's *unlikely* that a <u>concussion</u> or other brain injury has occurred. If the baby becomes pale and drowsy, starts to vomit, or has a seizure, *call the doctor or hospital immediately.*

The high-chair

No high-chair is tilt-proof. You can buy security straps that are attached to the kitchen table. Your child should also wear a harness while sitting in the high-chair.

Stairs

Stairs are exciting for children as soon as they can crawl. Unfortunately, stairs are also potentially dangerous. You need to install gates at the top *and* bottom of the stairs, because children can crawl up or down them. Gates should be at least 27-1/2 to 29-1/2 inches tall, measured from the bottom edge. The space between the bars should be less than 2-3/8 inches, and there should be no cross bar in the middle. The gate must open up or in — *not* toward the stairs.

Spiral staircases and stairs with open backs are accident traps. Small children can fall through the open spaces or get their head stuck. Close up the open areas as best you can, and be especially careful about keeping the gates secured at all times.

Still, it is wise to teach a baby how to get up and down regular staircases. If somebody forgets to close a gate one day, your child may be able to avoid a serious fall by knowing how to walk or crawl. You can mount a hand-rail or rope at child's height, for support. Of course, a young child shouldn't be allowed to be on the stairs alone for some time yet!

Windows

Every year, too many children fall out a window and suffer injuries. Children have a large head, compared to the rest of their body. This can make it easy for a child to lose his or her balance and fall over. Install locks at the top of the window. Window bars are also available, if you want to be able to air the room. No window locks are *completely* secure, but it takes time for small children to open them.

BURNS

Unfortunately, burns are common among infants and toddlers. Scalding accidents occur when a child pulls a pot or pan down from the stove, or manages to turn on the hot water, or touches a hot radiator or oven door. The most common burn injuries are caused by hot water or hot beverages. Turn pot handles away from the front of the stove.

Heat injuries are divided into three categories. With first-degree burns, the injury is superficial; the skin becomes red, but isn't seriously harmed. Second-degree burns develop blisters filled with fluid. Third-degree burns involve tissue deep under the skin; the extent of the damage becomes apparent only after a few days. First-degree burns — and usually second-degree burns — heal without leaving a visible scar.

Immediately after a first-degree or second-degree burn, immerse the wounded area completely in *cold running water* until it is no longer painful. This stops the burning process. Some experts recommend bathing the area in a mild soap solution with added ice cubes — but *don't* put ice cubes directly onto the wound. The burn should then be kept dry — either air-dried or covered by dry, sterile bandages. You can put an antibiotic spray or burn ointment on before applying the bandage. *Do not* cover the area with a raw egg yolk, butter, or oil!

When burns are deep or extensive, contact the doctor or hospital *immediately*. Burns on the palm of the hand or near the eyes always require a call, too. While waiting for the ambulance or ride, and on the way to the doctor's office or emergency room, have the child drink plenty of water (if he or she isn't nauseous). People lose a lot of fluids during the first hours after serious burn damage.

Hot drinks and water

When you have a baby on your lap, you'll notice that he or she may suddenly kick and wave the arms and feet. These movements are impossible to predict. Therefore, *never* hold a baby on your lap when you are drinking hot beverages. Friends and relatives should also be taught this rule!

Children's skin is very sensitive and more easily damaged than ours. Did you know that damages from burns can occur even at temperatures as low as 104 °F? So, the risk of your child being scalded is high. Adjust the thermostat of the hot water heater to 110 °F, and secure all faucet handles in some way. Most households keep the water unnecessarily hot. A hot bath doesn't need to be more than 100 °F.

FOREIGN OBJECTS

Digestive system

It's incredible what babies put into their mouth and swallow: buttons, coins, needles, glass, and more! Fortunately, the objects usually pass through the stomach and the intestines without causing damage. You *should* be concerned, however, if the swallowed object is sharp, breakable, or poisonous, or if your child shows any signs of pain. In any of those cases, the doctor should be contacted immediately. Otherwise, try to calm down and feed the child. Do not give suppositories unless the doctor tells you to; they can increase the chances of damage. Don't put your finger into your child's mouth, either. Check the baby's stools during the first few days to make sure the object has passed through.

Respiratory system

If your child coughs or chokes after having put an object into his or her mouth, it is very likely that the object has gotten stuck in the airways. This is confirmed when the child can't make any noise or his or her face turns blue. Make the child cough up the object right away, or expel it by holding the child's head down while thumping the upper part of the back fairly forcefully between the shoulder blades. If these actions fail, call the emergency number and rush the child to a hospital.

Nose and ears

Small paper balls, peas, and stones are some of the things young children find "fun" to insert into their nose. This can be dangerous. It's best to try to remove such objects immediately. If you wait, a foul-smelling, yellow, sometimes bloody material may leak out of the nose. If your child is old enough to cooperate, you may be able to show him or her how to blow forcefully through the nose to dislodge the object. *Do not* attempt to remove it with tweezers, because great care is needed to not push it farther in. It's generally best to let a doctor remove objects stuck in the nose.

Babies also insert small objects into the ears. These can be easily removed with small tweezers, but be careful not to push the object farther in.

Some innocent-looking items

Pacifiers should have a protective shield of 1-1/2 inches. Check frequently that the pacifier is undamaged and strong. A pacifier with a loose nipple can cause a baby to choke.

Peanuts and hard candies shouldn't be given to children under 4 years old. The little one can swallow wrong and the peanut can end up in the lungs. And, peanuts contain an oil that harms lung tissue. You should also wait to give the child grapes or nuts. Anything smaller than a pencil's eraser tip can be breathed into the lungs and can get stuck in the throat and choke the child.

Make sure that toys don't have loose parts that a baby can put into his or her mouth. Check the eyes and nose of dolls and stuffed animals, and keep the toys of older children separate. Most toys are marked with age limits.

POISONING

Remember that all medicines and household cleaning products should be kept beyond the reach of children, preferably in locked cupboards, and not at floor level. Even everyday things like vitamins and dish-washing liquid are very dangerous for small children. Keep one ounce of ipecac syrup in the house, but never use it unless a doctor tells you to.

OTHER INJURIES

Graze wounds

Scrapes, rug burns, and other graze wounds should be washed with plenty of clean, cool water and soap, or with a special cleansing remedy from the pharmacy. Let the wound air-dry and apply a dry, sterile bandage. If the wound doesn't become painful or red, and the bandage stays dry, keep a bandage on for 8 to 10 days. If the bandage becomes dirty, change the outer layer, but leave the layer nearest the wound intact.

Cuts

Cuts sometimes bleed profusely for the first few minutes, which gives the impression of a serious injury. Apply pressure to the cut for a few minutes with the cleanest material available — preferably a small sterile bandage — while washing away the blood around the area. Find out how large the wound really is. Often it is enough to apply a bandage straight to the wound while pressing the edges of the cut slightly together. Apply a strong, sterile bandage. If the wound continues to bleed, or its edges are separated by more than a little bit, contact the doctor or go to the hospital.

If any wound has a lot of dirt or other contaminants in it, seek immediate medical help to protect against the risk — even if it is small — for tetanus developing. If the wound is deep, it's important for a doctor to find out whether nerves or tendons have been damaged.

Fractures

The bones of infants and toddlers are flexible, like green tree branches. Fractures heal faster in children than in adults. However, you should always seek medical advice if you suspect a broken bone.

IN THE CAR

Never hold an infant or child on your lap in the car. No matter how careful you are, it's impossible to protect the child if you're in an accident. All children under age 4 should be secured in an age-appropriate car seat. From age 4 or 40 pounds, seat belts must be worn at all times.

Good car seats can be bought, rented, or borrowed from many stores, including some car repair shops or car rental agencies. Check that the seat is approved by the federal government. These seats have been tested and offer good security. More information about car seats is found on page 64.

Index

Resource Associations

The following associations may be able to provide you with helpful information about pregnancy, birth, and caring for your baby.

Association of Labor Assistants and
  Childbirth Educators (ALACE)
P.O. Box 382724
Cambridge, MA 02238
617-441-8660

International Childbirth Education
  Association (ICEA)
Box 20048
Minneapolis, MN 55420
612-854-8660

La Leche League International
961 Minneapolis Avenue
Franklin Park, IL 60131
800-La-Leche

National Association of Childbearing
  Centers (NCH)
Box 1, Rt. 1
Perkiomenville, PA 18074